CONNECTED
spirits

CONNECTED SPIRITS

friends and spiritual journeys

EDITED BY Andrew J. Weaver
AND Donald E. Messer

THE PILGRIM PRESS
CLEVELAND

DEDICATED TO

Carolyn and Bonnie

with love

The Pilgrim Press, 700 Prospect Avenue, Cleveland, Ohio 44115-1100
thepilgrimpress.com
© 2007 Andrew J. Weaver and Donald E. Messer

Scripture quotations, unless otherwise noted, are from the New Revised
Standard Version of the Bible, © 1989 by the Division of Christian Education
of the National Council of Churches of Christ in the United States of America
and are used by permission. Changes have been made for inclusivity.

⊛ Printed in the United States of America on acid-free paper that
contains post-consumer fiber.

10   09   08   07   06   5   4   3   2   1

Library of Congress Cataloging-in-Publication Data

Connected spirits : friends and spiritual journeys / edited by Andrew J.
Weaver and Donald E. Messer.
      p. cm.
   ISBN 978-0-8298-1716-4 (alk. paper)
   1. Friendship—Religious aspects—Christianity.   I. Weaver, Andrew J.,
1947–   I. Messer, Donald E.
BV4647.F7C65 2007
241'.6762—dc22   2007003049

CONTENTS

FOREWORD

As I write this I find myself between very different friends, but all friends nevertheless. My friend Ella, whom I have known since she was twelve years old and who a few years ago served as my secretary, just sent me word of the progress of her young child who is suffering from a brain birth defect. Almost at the same time I received word from friends Angela and Gary informing me that the support, love, and prayers of their many friends across the United Methodist Church, my own included, have given them incredible strength as they have dealt with their daughter Lindsay's recent grave illness. I have never met Angela or Gary or their daughter Lindsay, but I felt as much joy when they informed me of Lindsay's progress as I experienced when I heard from my longtime friend, Ella, about her son's slow but steady progress toward healing and wholeness. What brought me to this sense of being connected as friends with these persons, fully known and yet to be known?

I believe the connection of friendship has come in the sharing of human need and vulnerability. When her son became ill, Ella contacted all her closest friends and asked us to pray for him and for her and her family. When Lindsay confronted her own illness, her parents Angela and Gary in their despair wrote to United Methodists across the United States, known and unknown, desperately asking for prayers. They called us all friends and asked whether in a spirit of friendship we would join them in prayer for their daughter. In opening their hearts and lives, these persons welcomed me into the sacred bond of friendship. Friendships of prayer and witness to the mercy of God have blessed all of our lives.

This work on *Connected Spirits* blesses us as it invites us to pause and listen to deep and rich stories. Through it you may be as surprised as I was by the possibilities for friendship and thus the opportunity for living lives that are sustained and nurtured by friendship. It is impossible to hear such stories and not consider the friendships of our own lives, woven into the sinew of our existence and who we have become. In this way it is a book that encourages thoughtful reflection, thus creating an even greater resource as we add our stories of friendship to those we read about.

Much has been written about such matters as war and peace, love and hate, alienation and reconciliation, but what of friendship? We are reminded that Jesus seeks to be our friend. In the Gospel according to John, Jesus says to his disciples, "I do not call you servants any longer, because the servant does not know what the master is doing; but I have called you friends . . ." (John 15:15). Martin E. Marty tells us friendship is not an abstraction, but that which we climb into always seeing something of value in the other. There is no doubt that our friend Jesus sees something of value in each one of us and thus climbed right onto that cross of redemption and life.

What would happen if on our spiritual journeys we sought not only to find answers to the human struggles of our own making and those we have inherited, but also committed ourselves to cultivating and tenderly caring for friendships? Tender care would require speaking truth in love, self-giving, the suspension of judgment, waiting for each other, and going deep within ourselves to bring forth a goodness that inspires and heals and makes possible true and faithful friendships. A commitment to holy friendships of the abiding kind might just make us vulnerable enough to be able to receive God's own merciful love.

—*Bishop Minerva G. Carcaño*

Phoenix Episcopal Area
Desert Southwest Annual Conference
of the United Methodist Church

PREFACE

When Andrew Weaver, a colleague and friend, asked me to write a preface to this book, I accepted immediately. I said yes because I knew he would be pleased to have my support. I, however, was the one who benefited because this volume is an irresistible invitation to live differently.

This book enabled me to reflect on my many relationships. For example, reading that "Each meal is a loving gift" as prepared by a friend helped make what had been unconscious in me conscious. I can now call my mother-in-law, who always prepares meals for me and my wife, a friend. In fact, upon reflection, she is more of a friend to me than I to her. Indeed, we are surrounded by more friends than we might have recognized.

The numerous images of friends in this volume of sixteen essays have helped me to see the many faces of God in nature and in my friends: mentor, father, comrade, branch of a tree, birthing of each other, angels, stars, pearls, river, professor, neighbor, family by choice, children, and beautiful flowers.

What does holy friendship look like?

"This is my commandment, that you love one another as I have loved you. No one has greater love than this, to lay down one's life for one's friends. You are my friends if you do what I command you" (John 15:12–14). Jesus calls us friends if we do what is required of us—to love. When we express our love, we are friends of Jesus and we are friends of those who come in contact with us. Jesus revolutionized the notion of family to include the spiritual community of those who do the will of God (Matt. 12:46–50). To do God's will is to love by obeying the commandment—"If you love me, you will keep my commandments" (John 14:15). In the parable of the good Samaritan, Jesus redefines neighbor by transcending clan and proximity of residency to include persons who respond with loving action to those needing help (Luke 10:25–37). The call to be a neighbor is a call to be a friend in the context of love. These biblical texts are connected by the notion of love. It is no wonder that our neighbors, our mothers, our brothers, or even a stranger like the good Samaritan can be our friends.

As a prison chaplain in the New York City Correction Department for eleven years and one who has been given the nickname of "Chaplain Cool," I know that my position only gets me a face-to-face encounter with inmates. To be effective, however, I must relate to them not as a government official, but as a friend who is nonjudgmental, noncondemning, forgiving, while speaking the truth with love in order to create a context for repentance and transformation. The love of a friend can facilitate healing and forgiveness.

If the essence of friendship is love, the determining factor, it is understandable that relationships of parent-child, professor-student, pastor-parishioner, chaplain-inmate, spouses, colleagues, siblings, neighbors, and so on can be between true friends.

Extending the love of God to another friend transcends social location, financial status, racial designation, political allegiance, power differential, sexual orientation, religious affiliation, doctrinal differences, and stages of faith. When this happens, it is a meeting of equals, heart-to-heart, spirit-to-spirit, true self to true self. And what makes a friendship holy at a particular moment is that it is both loving and just.

When one cannot share deep pain with a friend, the friendship becomes superficial. When hurt by betrayal, we are reminded of Jesus treating Judas and Peter as friends in spite of their actions.

According to Webster's dictionary, a friend is "a person whom one knows well and is fond of; one who is not an enemy; a supporter, a friend in being helpful and reliable." Because friendship is both an emotional state and a spiritual connection due to love expressed and shared, it means one can be in and out of friendship at any given moment—friends become enemies and enemies become friends.

If genuine love is unconditional, accepting, self-emptying, and self-sacrificing, then friendship between two individuals is not necessarily equal in force. That is to say, "one person is more friend than the other." So if someone does not behave like a friend to you, it does not necessarily mean that you are not his or her friend. Jesus is a true friend to us, but that does not mean we are true friends to Jesus all the time. Nevertheless, there is a friendship. And it is the gift of the Spirit that binds friends together.

Befriend the enemy (love your enemy) with the hope that one day this enemy becomes a friend. When everyone, every country, loves each other as true friends, then the reign of God on earth is realized. True friendship offers hope for our conflicted, polarized world.

I want to give copies of this book to my friends, because it is a book of real people with real stories of goodness and betrayal, of sins and grace. This volume serves as a mirror to help us see where we are, and it functions as a window to what we can become as individuals and as a human race.

God blesses, challenges, and ministers to us through family and other persons. If we do not see them as friends, who are they to us?

See them each as your friend! Let us practice holy friendship together.

—*James Kam-Leung Law, D. Min.*

Senior pastor
Chinese United Methodist Church
New York, New York

ACKNOWLEDGMENTS

We are thankful to Bishop Minerva G. Carcaño of the Desert Southwest Area (Phoenix, Arizona) of the United Methodist Church for writing the forward for this volume. We are also grateful to Rev. James Kam-Leung Law of Chinese United Methodist Church in New York City for writing the preface for this book. A portion of the proceeds from this book will go to the United Methodist Committee on Relief for the AIDS Orphans Trust, a ministry in Africa.

We are grateful to Rev. Carolyn L. Stapleton for her invaluable help. Her exceptional editing and research skills added immeasurably to the quality of the text. We are thankful for her ministry. We are also appreciative of the assistance of Suk Ki Lee for her help in preparing the manuscript.

INTRODUCTION

Henri Nouwen noted the importance of friendships when he wrote: "We need loving and caring friends with whom we can speak from the depth of our heart. Such friends can take away the paralysis that secrecy creates. They can offer us a safe and sacred place, where we can express our deepest sorrows and joys, and they can confront us in love, challenging us to a greater spiritual maturity."[1] Researchers have found that most persons agree with Father Nouwen, in that people rank friendships among the things that matter most to them from childhood through adulthood.[2] Friends offer companionship, intimacy, emotional support, loyalty, trust, and fun.

Studies show that that during difficult times our friends are of particular value in sustaining our sense of well-being. College students who have quality long-term friendships report greater optimism and better adjustment to stressful life events.[3] An investigation of Puerto Rican and Dominican women rearing their grandchildren in New York City documented the important role of support from friends, church groups, and neighbors for meeting the emotional and social needs of daily life.[4] A national study examined stressful life events and alcohol use among adults sixty years of age and older. The results indicate that supportive resources of friends and church have a stress-buffering effect that reduces excessive drinking during a life crisis.[5]

The church is often a place where persons develop bonds with others. Among midwestern older adults who attended church regularly, it was discovered that the majority reported that 80 percent or more of their closest friends came from their congregation.[6] In a study of elders in southern Florida, investigators found that greater involvement in their faith community was significantly related to less loneliness and a stronger network of relationships.[7] Researchers have also found that a lack of friends and resultant loneliness have been linked in research to depression, anxiety, and a poor self-concept.[8]

The Catholic, United Methodist, Lutheran, United Church of Christ, and Episcopal contributors in this book have reflected on their experiences with friends as a part of their own faith journey: What spiritual lessons and wisdom can be shared from encounters with close friends? In what ways did these friendships foster spiritual maturity? How have friendships deepened our faith? How have friends given spiritual guidance during difficult times? How has the experience of betrayal by friends affected one's own spiritual life? In what ways have friends challenged us to a greater spiritual maturity?

We believe that readers will find these shared stories of friendship compelling as we have, and the results are a blessing.

Notes

1. Henri Nouwen, *Can You Drink the Cup?* (Notre Dame, Ind.: Maria Press, 1996).

2. F. E. Aboud, and M. J. Mendelson, "Determinants of Friendship Selection and Quality: Developmental Perspectives." In W. M. Bukowski, A. F. Newcomb, and W. W. Hartup, eds., *The Company They Keep: Friendship in Childhood and Adolescence* (New York: Cambridge University Press, 1996), 87–112.

3. I. Brissette, M. F. Scheier, and C. S. Carver, "The Role of Optimism in Social Network Development, Coping, and Psychological Adjustment during a Life Transition. *Journal of Personality & Social Psychology* 82/1 (2002): 102–11.

4. D. Burnette, "Social Relationships of Latino Grandparent Caregivers: A Role Theory Perspective. *Gerontologist* 39/1 (1999), 49–58.

5. K. M. Jennison, "The Impact of Stressful Life Events and Social Support on Drinking among Older Adults: A General Population Survey," 1992.

6. H. G. Koenig, D. O. Moberg, and J. N. Kvale, "Religious Activities and Attitudes of Older Adults in a Geriatric Assessment Clinic." *Journal of the American Geriatrics Society* 36 (1988): 362–74.

7. D. P. Johnson and L. C. Mullins, "Religiosity and Loneliness among the Elderly," *The Journal of Applied Gerontology* 8/1 (1989): 110–31.

8. B. T. McWhirter, "Loneliness: A Review of Current Literature with Implications for Counseling and Research," *Journal of Counseling and Development* 68 (1990): 417–23; R. O. Hansson, W. H Jones, B. N. Carpenter, and I. Remondet, "Loneliness and Adjustment to Old Age," *International Journal of Aging and Human Development* 24 (1986): 41–53.

ONE

TRANSCENDENT FRIENDSHIPS
The Journey to Spiritual Growth

ESTHER KWON ARINAGA

Afamiliar scene at my local public library greets me on a quiet Saturday afternoon: patrons sitting at blinking computers, searching for the key word that will open a cache of possibilities. I type "friendship," and within a few seconds the electronic card catalog produces a yield of five thousand-plus entries with an accompanying plea: narrow your search. I select nonfiction, confident that a large field of personal reflections on friendship will appear. It is not to be. Instead the computer unearths only twenty-four listings, mostly books about friendships involving artists, musicians, writers, and athletes. None hints of any spiritual connection. I could peruse five thousand other entries but decide first to look closely at the titles already before me.

REVELATIONS AND FRIENDSHIP
Among the two dozen books on "nonfiction friendship," one title is arresting: *The Teammates: A Portrait of a Friendship* by journalist/historian David Halberstam. I am intrigued. Is it is possible to capture on canvas or the printed page the nuances—the colors—of a friendship? Baseball had brought the four teammates together; they were Boston Red Sox players Ted Williams, Johnny Pesky, Dominic DiMaggio, and Bobby Doerr. The book jacket explains: "What Halberstam has given us is a book about baseball, and something more, the richness of friendship."[1] What was on the author's palette of friendship that produced a portrait of "richness?"

Most of us cannot imagine the strain of being with friends, day in and day out, in the clubhouse, on trains, in training camps, and through roller coaster seasons of wins and losses. Add to this mix stardom and bruised egos, game pressures and disappointing performances. It is a miracle that a friendship was able to flower and endure among the four baseball players. But closeness enables friends to be readily open to contact by telephone, e-mail, or an impulsive, sometimes desperate knock at the front door. With physical proximity, too, we are able to witness firsthand the impact on a friend of a major quarrel or even a trivial misunderstanding. A fair interpretation of the "facts" permits a more reasoned explanation of a friend's actions. Unlike the media, Ted Williams' friends understood his outbursts of temper and his frustration over negative stories—often uninformed—about his playing and his personal life. Good friends take the time and effort to differentiate between fact and fiction.

Most friendships require a long period of gestation. Halberstam observed that friendship among the Red Sox teammates took root only after they each allowed their friends to enter the depths and shallows of their personal lives. Ted Williams, who had had a sad and lonely childhood, found it difficult to reveal his past to his teammates. They waited patiently until he was finally ready to tell them about the misery and shame of his family life. In his poem "Revelation," Robert Frost speaks of our reluctance to tell all. "We make ourselves a place apart / Behind light words that tease and flout / But, oh, the agitated heart / Till someone really finds us out / . . . But so with all, from babes that play / At hide and seek to God afar / So all who hide too well away / Must speak and tell us where they are."[2]

Between or among friends the moment of revelation is sacred. When the burden of secrecy and concealment is lifted, we enter into a friend's most private realm. The integrity of a friendship is assured when a friend endows us with grace and trust.

Not all revelations among friends are dramatic, but I have learned they can transcend the ordinary and raise the bar of friendship. In 1976 I was hired as the executive director of a small nonprofit organization facing serious financial and personnel problems. On the hiring committee was a young woman with whom I felt immediate rapport. During ensuing months we met weekly over lunch to discuss the challenges facing the agency. We discovered that we shared many interests—a love of literature and art, a passion for Asian history and culture, and a rabid interest in politics. Our conversations were animated, exhilarating, and probably could have gone on for hours each time. During a lull in conversation one day I looked across the table and found Sarah (not her real name) staring absently at her plate. She looked up and quietly asked, "What if I told you that I'm black, an African American?"

I was speechless.

Seeing my look of surprise at her revelation, Sarah quickly explained that in Georgia, her place of birth, "Anyone—black or white—walking down the street would know at a glance that I'm African American. My parents have very dark skin, my brother and sisters, too. I'm the only one who's a mulatto." Sarah hardly resembled the image of a mulatto that I had seen depicted in magazines when I was a child. With her fair hair, light complexion, and blue-green eyes, Sarah looked haole, a white person in Hawaii.

I mumbled something inane. "I would have never guessed."

As Sarah spoke, my thoughts were racing; I wondered why she felt it was necessary to reveal her racial background. Why did it matter? Had I said something to her that may have been offensive or biased? I was afraid to question her further, afraid to invade Sarah's private world, and afraid that any further discussion might lead to awkward feelings between us. My own background seemed so transparent, in part because Sarah was already familiar with my vitae and employment history. She knew my background as a Korean American, but I realized that I knew very little about Sarah's distant past.

Misunderstandings are bound to arise between friends of different racial or ethnic backgrounds. Language, customs, and cultural practices shape an individual's Weltanschauung; so on occasion friends need an interpretation or a translation. In these instances perhaps a series of revelations must occur before friends can reach a place where differences are openly discussed, embraced, and celebrated. When Sarah revealed her racial background, it was her first revelation. Despite our closeness I realized that we were still "digging" the roots of our friendship.

Several years would pass before we were able to transcend this stage of friendship. One summer I was enrolled in an expository writing course that required students to write an essay based on an interview of a friend. Sarah was home on leave from her post as an officer in the

Foreign Service. We were eager to resume our marathon conversations. I asked Sarah if she were willing to be the subject of my essay. She was reluctant but finally agreed if I promised not to use her real name.

We met in my apartment early in the afternoon, two old friends resuming a friendship after a year's separation. I turned on the tape recorder. First, questions about her family; then about her childhood in Atlanta; followed by glimpses of her educational background and the journey to find her place "on the planet." Sarah described the invisible line drawn around her African American community. She was not allowed to cross that line into "white" territory, even if it offered a shortcut to her destination. Sarah's pale complexion had set her apart from her playmates. They were unkind, in the way children can be when confronting someone who looks different from them. At times they excluded her; she was not one of them. There were instances when Sarah wished she were black, so she could fit in. At other times she felt her friends envied her fair skin, perhaps suggesting that being different was an advantage she had over them.

Sarah's voice trembled when she remembered the admonitions of "Negro elders" who warned their children and grandchildren about the dangers of "stirring the wrath of white folks." The 1955 abduction, murder, and mutilation of a young boy, Emmitt Till, just because "he whistled at a white woman" had spread terror throughout African American communities in the South. For years, Emmitt Till was a symbol of the potential for white cruelty to unsuspecting children.

A few years ago the Public Broadcasting System retold the story of Till's murder. Widespread media coverage in America told the story of bigotry and cruelty to a new audience. None of these news stories could compare to Sarah's telling of that terrible killing. I will never forget the fear etched on her face and the stuttering emotion of her voice as she connected memory and words.

More than three hours later, I turned off the tape recorder. The room was still. For a long while no words passed between us. Sarah is an avowed agnostic, but I believe she felt as I did that we had had an intense spiritual experience. I thought I understood at last why she had wanted me to know who she really was. The color of pain may be red or black, but whatever its hue, pain occupies a space on the palette of a friendship. Just as Ted Williams finally revealed his story of shame and embarrassment to his teammates, Sarah had shared with me the humiliation and intense suffering she had endured during her youth in the segregated South. She had had a relatively happy childhood within her own family and community and had achieved success in her career, but the evil of segregation and the complexities of appearing white though black had remained deeply recessed within her soul.

The interview with Sarah offered an opportunity for intimacy previously missing in our friendship—a friendship that continues to grow in maturity as we laugh, cry, celebrate, and rail at injustice. We have shared our deepest fears, especially during the medical crises our spouses have undergone. We have spoken often of the interview. Sarah reminds me that whenever she feels discouraged, she rereads my essay. It comforts, connects, and reaches across time and space.

MENTORS

Between friends, revelations open doors to the soul, but in my experience mentoring by a friend enables the Holy Spirit to enter the heart and mind. Mentors are evident in a variety of professional venues today: a senior professor advises a promising doctoral candidate; an executive guides a rising corporate star; a coach or sports agent takes a talented athlete under his wing. But these are not necessarily relationships based on friendship.

In Greek mythology Mentor was a wise and trusted friend, a counselor to Odysseus. Mentor more closely resembles friends who have influenced my journey of faith. Spiritual mentors listen and hear. They have the innate ability to sense the angst of the person before them. They are open to friendship, even if a vast difference exists in age, status, or education. Mentors often become lifelong friends.

Pastors in a local church are important mentors, especially to those who are entering young adulthood. I was seventeen when World War II ended. The early postwar years brought rapid changes on the national and local level. In my own small world an unexpected tragedy occurred when my mother was struck and killed by a teenager driving a truck. As in many Asian families, my mother was the hub of our family, the nurturer, and the transmitter of our Korean culture. Her sudden loss was palpable. My father was grieving and understandably grew distant. By letter I then learned that my closest high school friend who was attending college in Wisconsin was diagnosed with leukemia; she passed away a few months later. The First Korean Methodist Church that I had attended all my life was suddenly uprooted to make way for urban redevelopment in downtown Honolulu. Our pastor tried valiantly to keep the flock together in a two-story frame house—our temporary chapel until the new church could be built. Members began moving away to new churches in rapidly developing postwar suburbs. Our church's bilingual service had never satisfied those of us in the second generation. Now meeting in a cramped living room of an old house seemed to exacerbate our discontent.

I felt spiritually bereft. My world seemed to be falling apart. Loss and loneliness seemed to go hand in hand.

A college friend and I decided to visit other churches. Our first stop was a Methodist church that had decided not to relocate from the inner city. Harris Memorial Methodist Church, like the First Korean Methodist Church, was chartered by immigrants. Most of the members were of Japanese ancestry, including its pastor, Dr. Harry Komuro. The pastor's gentle manner and slight build did not prepare me for his almost stentorian delivery of the sermon. We met after the service, and Harry (it took many years before I could drop his more formal title) invited me to visit him during the week.

From our first meeting I was drawn to Harry's spiritual depth. We met every week in his small, comfortable study next to the church. We prayed together, read the Bible, talked about family and college, and explored a wide range of ideas. Psalm 121, one of the first scriptures we read together, became a bulwark—a safeguard—for me in times of crisis. I can still remember the warmth of the late afternoon sun streaming through the study window. Occasionally, Harry's little daughter danced through the room in her tutu and ballerina shoes. He would simply smile. Many decades later, when Harry was in his early nineties, we would talk on the telephone. Shortly before his passing, I reminded him of our days together in his study and told him once again how much they had meant to me. A few days later I received a note in his own handwriting, telling me how my words had given him such joy. Harry's mentoring was without end.

Harry and I began our friendship simply as pastor and parishioner, but as my mentor and friend, Harry showed me the way to spiritual maturity.

The decision to leave my childhood church was not easy, but my pastor and my father both encouraged me to transfer my membership to Harris Church. Like Harry, they recognized that my spiritual life was in crisis. Their approval came at some cost to them personally. Koreans in Hawaii were still bitter about Japan's occupation of Korea for thirty-five years. Enmity toward the Japanese persisted despite the end of World War II and the liberation of Korea. Many older Koreans remembered the persecution of Christians under colonial rule. When church members heard about my "defection" to "the Japanese church," they chastised both my father and our pastor. But freedom to choose was an important ideal for my father. It was the principal reason he decided to immigrate to America in 1905.

Immigrants played an important role as mentors in the church of my childhood. I was always fascinated by Dora Kim Moon. She was a devout Christian and one of the founding members of the First Korean Methodist Church in Honolulu at the turn of the twentieth century. Dora was an imposing figure during church services and meetings. It was said that she was the only woman whose counsel the men in the church would follow. Dora's entire life was dedicated to Christian service. She was a deacon, a mentor to women in need, and a fund-raiser for families of ministers imprisoned in Korea. As a small child, I was fascinated by Dora even though I could barely understand her. She spoke little English.

Dora was baptized at the Methodist Mission in Pyongyang in the late nineteenth century. After her baptism she received an ultimatum from her father-in-law: "Give up being a Christian or leave the house immediately." On a snowy January evening, carrying her young daughter on her back, Dora left her husband, her home, and her traditional life in Korea. Missionaries at the mission gave her refuge. With their help she became a Bible woman, a woman of Christian faith who accompanied a group of immigrants traveling by ship to Hawaii in 1904. The men in the group were under contract to work on sugar plantations in Hawaii. Dora converted many of them to Christianity during the long voyage.

After leaving my childhood church, I did not see Dora for several years until we met at a social event. Despite her age Dora displayed the same inner strength and resolve, and a radiance that had always enthralled me. I was to be married in a few months, and I think Dora sensed that I missed my mother and the other women of her church who had been my extended family. Dora invited me to visit her later that week. For almost a year we met weekly in her home. Anyone observing us would have been perplexed by our "conversations." Dora still spoke little English. My level of Korean was still that of a second-grade student.

Each Friday afternoon Dora greeted me at the door and offered a rare smile. She was always elegantly dressed. We sat side by side on the living room sofa, two women separated in age by nearly fifty years. Dora's hands clasped her well-worn Bible. She knew many verses by heart. With my limited Korean, it was a struggle to keep up. Often we sat quietly, enjoying the stillness. Such moments brought us closer to each other in spirit and into God's presence. Each time before I took leave, Dora grasped both of my hands in hers and offered a silent prayer. I learned from Dora that faith grows even in the absence of words.

BONDING IN CHURCH

Friendships we make in church present unique challenges. Members meet before the weekly service begins and briefly after church, at the front door or in the social hall. Conversations are hurried and usually interrupted as we seek to greet friends. Another seven days will pass before we return to church. If we sing in the choir or serve on a committee or take on a leadership role, we may have more opportunities to get "to know all about" a fellow church member, especially if we remain members of a congregation for a long period. My husband Clifford and I unfortunately are "nomads"—we have changed our residence at least fifteen times over five decades of marriage. Frequent moves have led to memberships in many different types of churches in varying locales: large downtown edifices, suburban neighborhood churches, and country village-like parishes.

Joining a new church every four or five years presents a challenge, one that admittedly becomes more difficult as Clifford and I grow older. All churches, even those of the same denomination, are not equal. Pastoral "styles," the order of worship, and church administration vary widely. The backgrounds and ages of members are diverse in one church and relatively homogeneous in another. A major challenge always is to determine the spiritual maturity—if it exists—of a church and its members. A recent experience helped me realize that faith and friendship grow when members begin to bond spiritually.

Seven years ago Clifford and I joined a small suburban Methodist church. The predominance of older members made us feel at home. We liked the youthful pastor, the intimacy of the setting with its magnificent stained glass window above the altar, and the friendliness of the congregation. We became active on several committees. A few years later our pastor was reassigned after serving nearly thirteen years. Problems arose soon after the arrival of the new minister.

Pastoral differences with a congregation are not unusual, especially after the long tenure of a prior minister. But within a year our church faced a crisis; long-time members began leaving. Many who departed had held leadership positions, including membership on the personnel committee. Church attendance dwindled by 40 percent. Because I had served on personnel committees in other churches, I was hurriedly asked to join the depleted committee. Our task was monumental: to decide whether to ask that the pastor of our church be replaced or whether to stay on the same course and hope for a miracle.

Most members of the personnel committee had belonged to the church for many years. Several, who had already spent a year wrestling with the problem, were showing signs of agitation and anger. But from the first meeting of the reorganized committee, I sensed each member's deep loyalty to the church and the desire to "do the right thing." At every meeting and in all of our e-mails and telephone calls, we continually spoke of the need to pray for guidance. We asked ourselves questions: What would Jesus have advised in this situation? Is saving the church of greater importance than protecting our minister from eventual hurt and possible professional injury? How can we reconcile our feelings of conflict? We struggled for weeks. We sought guidance from higher officials but we knew that ultimately we had to recommend a resolution. Having taken a vow of confidentiality, we felt an enormous burden of responsibility.

I watched the drama unfold over two long months. Slowly members of the committee realized that we were witnessing a remarkable demonstration of Christian love and friendship. Relief came when we finally reached our decision. It was not without emotional pain. We decided that saving the church was our first priority.

Toward the end of our harrowing experience, an exhausted committee member said that many times she felt we were on a rowboat, paddling against a strong current toward an unknown destination.

Somehow we all knew that we would reach a safe harbor with God's grace and direction. Our trust in God, the support we gave one another when spirits lagged, and the bonds of friendship forged during our ordeal had all enabled us to achieve a spiritual maturity we had never before experienced.

. . .

When I began to look back on the friendships I have had over the past eight decades, I noticed a pattern emerging. Despite periods of separation and impediments, certain friendships endured, while others fell by the wayside. We live in a world where time is increasingly considered a valuable commodity that must be hoarded. But in friendships that survive the constraints of time, one party or both will use her time, her energy, and her wisdom to maintain the relationship. Making a telephone call, writing an e-mail or personal note, sharing a meal, taking the initiative to counsel and to be a mentor, listening closely and quietly to another's heartbeat or heartbreak—these are simple acts of kindness that help friends on their journey of faith. Spiritual growth awaits their arrival.

Notes

1. David Halberstam, *The Teammates: A Portrait of a Friendship* (New York: Hyperion, 2003), dust jacket copy.

2. Robert Frost, "Revelation," in Robert Frost, *A Boy's Will* (New York: Henry Holt and Company, 1915); Bartleby.com, 1999. www.bartleby.com/117/.

TWO

THEY HAVE BEEN THERE FOR ME

JAMES ARMSTRONG

K arl Jaspers once wrote that our "supreme achievement in this world is communication from personality to personality."[1] We are fashioned in the image of a personal God and the core of our beings is self-transcendent. We live in a relational world. Our personhoods are molded and shaped as we interact with those about us. Their graces and strengths have made them irreplaceable companions of the way. How profoundly grateful I am for friends and family who have shared my dreams and struggles—and the journey continues. In Madrid's Prado there hangs the painting of an old, old man leaning on a cane. Underneath is the caption: *Aun aprendo*—I'm still learning. Human development is a never-ending process. We are, each of us, works in progress.

PARENTS AS FRIENDS

For me it began in 1924. I was born in the Grant County Hospital in Marion, Indiana. My mother, a former school teacher, was prim and proper, gentle, intelligent, sensitive, artistic, and deeply religious. I can still hear her quiet voice as she prayed; her lovely soprano voice as she and my father sang duets. She was an "ideal preacher's wife" as people used to say. But, she was so much more than that. I was a sickly youngster and she spent endless hours caring for me while teaching me "numbers" and how to read and write. Those were Depression years and our little family was not exempted from the hardship and desperation that plagued the lives of millions of Americans. Hers was the stubborn faith that held us together.

If Mother was the ideal preacher's wife, Dad was anything but a typical preacher. Growing up in the rough 'n' tumble of western Montana, his best friend was the saloonkeeper's son. His first serious fling was the saloonkeeper's daughter. He had his nose broken three times—football, baseball, and boxing. As a member of Montana's National Guard, he was sent to New Mexico to ward off Pancho Villa and his band of Mexican revolutionaries.

Years later, when I entered his world, he had mellowed. As I wrote in my *Feet of Clay on Solid Ground*, "He was a loveable bear of a man who was equally at home wearing an apron in the kitchen, helping farmers with their plowing, tucking a toothpick into the back of his mouth as he kissed his little boy good night, or brawling with a hardware merchant who called him a 'sonofabitch.' He was tempestuous, warm hearted, good natured, a rebellious sort of maverick who was never far beyond the reach of his loved ones."[2] He was an excellent preacher, a marvelous pastor, and as tough as nails; quite a role model for a growing boy.

When, at the ripe old age of seventeen, I "had to get married," I am sure I broke my parents' hearts. There were no histrionics, no judgmental tirades. I never saw the tears I am certain they shed. Their love was unconditional and they stood by and supported me and my child bride, Phyllis Jeanne (she was seventeen too). If the words "holy friends" can be applied to anyone they can most certainly be applied to my parents.

Phyllis and I, with our little family, moved from southern California to Florida. Graduating from Florida Southern College, I went to Candler School of Theology in Atlanta. While there my father, only fifty-eight, had a cerebral hemorrhage and was suddenly gone.

A "HOLY" MENTOR

P. M. Boyd received us into his church in St. Petersburg. He led me toward the ministry and, as superintendent of the Tampa District of the Methodist Church, signed my license to preach in 1945. When Dad died Boyd wrote, "I can never take the place of your own father, but I could never be more devoted to you or take more pride in your ministry if you were my own son." When I graduated from seminary he asked me to join him as his associate at the First Methodist Church of Jacksonville. There followed three of the most instructive and rewarding years of my life. I learned more from him about pastoral care and "running a church" than from all of the textbooks I had read and graduate schools I had attended. I was elected to the episcopacy in 1968. He flew to Peoria to join the laying-on-of-hands ceremony. He died on October 5, 1975. At his funeral I said that though others had been a part of the consecration service in Peoria "it was Dick Boyd's hand that, for me, provided the apostolic succession."

I dedicated my first book, *The Journey That Men Make* (the sexist title was taken from a James Michener quotation) to Dr. Boyd. He received an advance copy, read my tribute, and mentioned the tears than coursed down his cheeks. He wrote of the "privilege of walking part of the journey with [me]—flesh of my flesh, blood of my blood, bone of my bone, soul of my soul." We did not always agree about matters of faith and church policy, but we corresponded at least once a month for more than twenty years and I will always be grateful for the gifts of grace he so freely gave me.

Boyd was as straight-laced (apart from an occasional off-color joke) as a person could be, but how he did love people and respond to their needs. He seemed shockproof. No human frailty caught him off guard. His capacity to be one with the errant youth, the grieving widow, the broken and discredited public official, or the foul-smelling panhandler was almost beyond belief. It would be something of a stretch to call many of my valued friends "holy," but of them all, Boyd was the holiest by far (with the probable exception of Wenonah Hatfield, but more of her later).

"HOLY" FRIENDS IN THE CONGREGATION

In 1958 we left Florida and moved to Indianapolis. I was named senior minister of the thirty-three-hundred-member Broadway Methodist Church. The ten years I served Broadway were the most heartwarming and satisfying years of my pastoral ministry. At Broadway a very special breed of mortal saints became my friends and spiritual mentors. There were many, but standing out from among the others were Lester Bill, Parker Pengilly, and Wenonah Hatfield. Lester was at Broadway when I arrived. He was my associate pastor and remains my dear though distant friend. A man with deep devotional roots, he was a truly spiritual man. At the same time he was one of those Henry Wallace kind of Iowa radicals. He was a pacifist. He led groups to Russia when it was still the Soviet Union. He took folks to the United Nations in New York. He and his family lived in Crosstown, an African American section of the inner city across Fall Creek from our church. He, his wife, and his three growing children would lead neighborhood clean-up campaigns. They would scrub walls and paint rickety frame houses. They would mimeograph and distribute neighborhood newsletters. At a time when Indianapolis was seething with racial unrest, he and his family lived the gospel. He will never know how much I admired and learned from him.

Parker Pengilly, a Republican attorney and son of a parson, chaired the search committee that brought me to Broadway. When I met with him in his downtown office and saw framed pictures of Lincoln and Gandhi on his wall I felt I had found a soul mate. Later he would be deeply involved in our neighborhood ministries. (The Mapleton–Fall Creek neighborhood numbered about seventeen thousand people. When we arrived in 1958, it was white. When we left, ten years later, it was 85 percent black.) He chaired the church's Urban Life Committee, a marvelous group of people that oversaw our outpost Sunday schools, our Friday night teen canteen, a thrift shop, a health clinic, a well-baby clinic, a Planned Parenthood clinic, Head Start classes that utilized church space on weekdays, and an after school program that featured remedial reading groups, sewing and cooking classes, Bible study and recreation—programs that reached more than four hundred youngsters each week. In his quiet, unassuming way, Parker convinced me that it was possible to be a Republican and a faithful, color-blind, sleeves-rolled-up servant of Christ at the same time. During these days of neoconservative madness I need to be reminded of that.

Wenonah Hatfield lived, with her old and crippled mother, in the same Crosstown neighborhood where Lester and Jane Bill lived. She had quit her job as a legal secretary, taken a drastic pay cut, and become one of our church secretaries. Every Thursday night she and her mother opened their home for a community prayer meeting. There was nothing stilted or formal about Wenonah's prayer life. Rather, the indwelling Spirit was her constant companion. She literally practiced the Presence. She gathered clothing for the children of a prostitute who lived next door. Her phone rang through the night as needy people called seeking a listening ear and prayerful counsel.

One Sunday afternoon Wenonah saw four little African American children playing in front of her house. She invited them in, fed them cookies and Kool-Aid, and told them Bible stories. That was the beginning of Broadway's Outpost Sunday School, a program that met in several homes and touched more than one hundred children every week. For seven years Wenonah was at the heart of the program, taking her youngsters to the zoo, to ball games, to restaurants. They became her very special family.

Shortly after we left Indianapolis, Wenonah died. After struggling more than two years she quietly succumbed to breast cancer. Her mother was there, in her wheelchair by her side, as she slipped away. The neighbors—all black, remember—wrote a letter to Mrs. Hatfield. I read it as a part of her memorial service:

> We, the neighbors of Winthrop Avenue, wish to express our deepest and heartfelt sympathy. We would like for you to know that we have lost a friend, a friend indeed. A friend that comes along once in a lifetime. But our loss is sure heaven's gain. We are proud to have known her for her Christian work and her saintly way of living. We saw her daily and not one time did we see her without that smile that only a child of God could wear.
>
> She was the founder of the children's Sunday school in our neighborhood that started in her home and grew so rapidly that more teachers and homes had to be used. Never was it too cold or too hot to see her going about the neighborhood winning children's hearts to Jesus. Dear ones in Christ, we could go on and on telling of the good things she stood for. But in closing may we say: sleep, sleep our loved one, and we will carry on as you wish.

Lester Bill, Parker Pengilly, Wenonah Hatfield—they wrote no books, led no workshops or seminars; they were not widely known and had no claim to fame, yet they taught me more about servanthood and genuine devotion, than all the headline grabbers I have known. They were, in every sense of the words, "holy friends."

"HOLY" STEADFAST FRIENDS DURING LIFE'S DARK DAYS

In 1968 I became a United Methodist bishop and served for fifteen years in that capacity. I chaired national boards and commissions. In the early 1980s I was president of the National Council of Churches. In May of 1982, *U.S. News and World Report* called me "the most influential religious leader in the United States." Then the bottom dropped out. Involved in an inexcusable extramarital affair, I resigned as president of the National Council and as a bishop of the United Methodist Church, opening my resignation statement with the words, "I am absolutely responsible for all that follows. I have been unfaithful to my wife and family."

In 2004, the movie *Sideways* was a surprising box-office hit. It chronicled a wine-tasting trip two friends made through the wine-growing regions of central California. The film told of the remarkable friendship of Jack, a washed-up actor who was about to be married, and of Miles, his long-suffering friend, who ran repeated risks for Jack, was humiliated by him, made sacrifices for him, and who forgave his many, costly foibles (and they were substantial). Although there was nudity, drunkenness, and profanity in the film, there were also some near sacred moments as the story drew to a close. In spite of everything, Miles offered the sleazy and deceitful Jack the gift of his steadfast friendship. During the dark days following October, 1983, I experienced the grace of friends like Miles. I had failed them in so many ways, but they were there for me.

Supportive warmth and understanding came from unexpected quarters. Cardinal Joseph Bernardin of Chicago and Fr. Ted Hesburgh of Notre Dame reached out with words of reassurance. Finus Crutchfield, a fellow United Methodist bishop, phoned. Crutchfield was a religious, social, and political conservative. We seldom agreed on matters of substance when the Council of Bishops met. However, I once stood with him as he faced a time of personal crisis, and, when I resigned, he called to offer me "any church in Texas"—not a very realistic or appealing option at the time.

More significant, however, were long-time friends who never flinched or wavered: Donald Messer, Rhett Jackson, and R. Benjamin Garrison were three such men. I first knew Don when he was completing his Ph.D. at Boston University. He returned to South Dakota, and I appointed him associate minister of the largest church in the Dakotas Area. Two or three years later I served on the committee that steered him into the presidency of Dakota Wesleyan University. Later he would be named president of Iliff School of Theology. We became good friends during those years, staying in touch, sharing dreams and confidences.

As I acknowledged my moral failures and prepared to resign my positions in the church, I kept Don informed. United Methodist seminary presidents and deans were meeting in San Francisco in October, 1983, alongside the Council of Bishops. Don became a conduit, my contact with the Council, sharing my desires and concerns with my colleagues —and theirs with me.

After those tortuous days, wanting to avoid the glare of publicity, I headed west, driving from Indianapolis to Denver and the home of Don and Bonnie Messer. They, with their youngsters, Christine and Kent, offered a place of anonymous refuge. If I chose to talk, attempting to think through my dilemma, they would listen. If I chose to brood and search my soul, they would leave me alone and provide a shield of silence. I was with them for nearly a month, a time of necessary introspection and recovery.

A few months later, Messer would write a column for *The United Methodist Reporter,* asking the church to offer "compassion, a spirit of redemption and reconciliation" to Phyllis and me. Later still he invited me to participate in the Iliff Week of Lectures, reflecting on my resignation. I spoke from the pulpit of the University Park United Methodist Church to a standing-room-only crowd of clergy and lay people who gave me an unbelievably warm reception. In a sense it was a coming-out party, my first self-conscious steps back into the parent church that had nurtured me from childhood on. In September 1985, following the death of preaching professor Ronald Sleeth, I was asked to become Visiting Professor of Preaching at Iliff, where I taught for six fruitful and wonderfully satisfying years. In 2000, I returned to the Iliff campus as Don stepped down as president of Iliff. We continue to stay in touch. As a dear friend, Donald Messer has stood with me every step of the way.

Rhett Jackson, known as "the Happy Bookseller" in Columbia, South Carolina, and across the country (he once chaired the national booksellers' association), is one of the truly great Christian laymen in

America. During the early 1960s he was part of a team that toured the southland pleading for an end to Methodism's Central ("Jim Crow") Jurisdiction. That vestige of a racist past was eliminated in 1968, and Rhett played a vital role in that necessary but belated transition. I first knew Rhett when I became president of the church's Commission on Religion and Race, and he was a key member and officer of the group. We were drawn to one another almost immediately. We celebrated our "double nickel" (fifty-fifth birthdays) together and spent valued time with each other.

In 1983, when my world fell apart, he was there. United Methodism's General Conference met in Baltimore in 1984. Some of my close friends would be in attendance. Rhett and Don Messer asked them to come together and asked me to join them. I did. It was a confessional, emotional moment. We talked openly and candidly about my "fall," my current state of mind, and my future plans (none had taken specific shape). The session was a profoundly meaningful gesture, and a practical step forward.

Rhett and I continue to stay in constant touch. We swap articles and ideas. We correspond a couple of times a month (e-mail is a marvelous thing). We have been in one another's homes. He has met with my seminary classes. We console one another in times of loss and laugh together on more cheerful days. I cherish the strong bonds that bind our lives together.

R. Benjamin Garrison was "Dicky Ben" when I first knew him. I was "Jimmie." Our fathers, ministerial friends, served churches just six miles apart. Our families were close and Dicky Ben and I spent part of our early childhood growing up together. Then, as our fathers moved on, our families drifted apart. He would go to Illinois Wesleyan and to Drew. I would go to Florida Southern and to Candler. When I moved from Florida to Indiana in 1958, Ben was serving the large and influential First Methodist Church in Bloomington. The years had seemed to make little difference and our friendship picked up where it had left off. We would meet and visit frequently. He would move on to the university church in Urbana, Illinois, and to churches in Lincoln and Lexington, Nebraska. I would leave Broadway to serve as bishop of the Dakotas Area, and later the Indiana Area. I would preach and lead retreats for him. He would come to the Dakotas and take part in our Pastors' Schools (his uncle, Edwin Garrison, had been my episcopal predecessor in the Dakotas). He would proof-text my manuscripts and

I would read and comment on his writing efforts. And all the while we would talk about changing the world, gossip about church politics, play table tennis, puff on our pipes, and share the intimate details of our lives. He knew me as no other person did. In my autobiography *Feet of Clay on Solid Ground*, I wrote:

> Garrison had been the prime mover back of my election to the episcopacy, had joined Dr. Boyd and the bishops in the laying-on-of-hands ceremony at my Service of Consecration in Peoria, and preached my installation sermon in Indianapolis in October, 1980. My "fall" would bring him greater pain than almost anyone apart from my immediate family.[2]

As I drove west toward Denver and the Messer home following my resignation, it was only natural for me to stop and spend a couple of days with Ben and Betty Garrison in Nebraska. My first night there Senator George McGovern of South Dakota tracked me down and called to offer words of comfort and warm support.

As the years passed Ben and I remained close after we both retired. Although separated by hundreds of miles, we exchanged phone calls every few weeks, and as the aging process took its toll and his health began to fail, the calls became more frequent. Finally he suffered respiratory failure and passed away. In 2002, I dedicated *Feet of Clay on Solid Ground* "to the memory of R. Benjamin Garrison, a lifelong friend and colleague."

"HOLY" FRIENDS IN LIFE'S CONTINUING JOURNEY

I left Iliff in 1991, when I was called to serve as senior minister at First Congregational Church in Winter Park, Florida. I retired from the pastoral ministry in 1999. My wife and I retain our membership in the Winter Park church and have become associate members of the Joy Metropolitan Community Church in Orlando. The senior ministers of both churches are former students of mine. My teaching ministry continues at Rollins College and the Florida Center for Theological Studies. My life has come full circle and even now my days are spilling over with gratitude and a deep sense of personal fulfillment.

And friends? *Aun aprendo* as they continue to teach, exemplify, and inspire. They include Jim Grant, who has been a part of my journey for more than fifty years and who continues to do what he can to keep me intellectually honest, Jim Wall, editor emeritus of *The Christian Century*, who helped see me through the roughest storms I encountered and who continues to reach out with words of encouragement, and Prakash Sethi, who became a valued colleague as we worked together in a Washington-based conflict resolution firm following my resignation, and who is now University Distinguished Professor at City University of New York. He has written textbooks I use in my classes, has come to Florida to meet with my students, and far more importantly, has shared the ins and outs of my personal journey over these past twenty years. We have been to India and South Korea together, have lectured from the same platforms, and have spent long hours discussing social problems, the clash of cultures, the insights of Hinduism and Christianity, and the joys of growing children and loving families.

Jim Allison came into my life after we arrived in Winter Park. The former head of the NAACP in central Florida, he was one of the founders of Bridgebuilders, devoting himself to bringing the black and white sections of our community together. He was a nagging presence in corridors of power as he raised his voice on behalf of the unwashed and the unwanted. We became comrades, fighting the good fight and having fun together. A series of strokes took him from us, but the community in which I live will never be the same because he passed this way.

Last, but far from least, there is Sharon Lynn, my Sheri. For the past several years she has shared every detail of my life. She has demonstrated the meaning of utter selflessness and true devotion. She has encouraged me in my professional pursuits, has widened the horizons of my mind (from cosmology and environmental politics to TV's "Iron Chef"), and has been by my side through the valleys and shadow lands of serious illness. She, as so many of these others, has been there for me.

COSTLY FRIENDSHIP

So, how have friends helped shape my journey? They have taught me that friendship is costly. Compassionate servanthood is the most basic of human virtues. Spirituality and authentic humanness are one. If holiness is not worldly it is irrelevant. There can be no love without justice; no justice without love. Penitence and forgiveness lead to understanding, acceptance, and new life.

Friends have prodded me, chastened me, inspired me, and enabled me to overreach myself. They have not only provided blessed memories, they have lifted me up, bade me stand, and enabled me to face and seize the futures that are yet before me.

NOTES

1. Karl Jaspers, *Way to Wisdom*, R. Manheim, translator (New Haven, Ct.: Yale University Press, 1973, original work published in England, 1951), 71.

2. James Armstrong, *Feet of Clay on Solid Ground* (Charleston, S.C.: BookSurge Publishing, 2002), 77.

THREE

SEE THEM EACH AS YOUR FRIEND

PASCHAL BAUMSTEIN

It was in watching my father that I first perceived that interplay of care and concern that is imperative in forging friendships. Father's rite for this effort operated without conscious protocol, I think. Whatever its design—or lack of design—however, his procedure worked. Yet it was never really his method that caught my attention. For me, the revelatory aspect of Father's friendships lay in where they found their substance.

Father was an exuberant angler and was always anxious to share this passion with others. So, through the years, relative after relative, guest after guest, would-be friend after would-be friend, found him- or herself induced to accompany him on predawn fishing trips. Each of these inexperienced and unsuspecting companions, on the appointed day, joined him uncomfortably in a roughly hewn rowboat, enveloped in darkness. Then, as Father's line (alone) harvested a bounty of malodorous bass, his guest—ordinarily he took just one companion at a time—would be left with little more to contemplate than the allure of sleep (or perhaps escape) and the unanticipated olfactory burdens of the morning's catch.

Of the various surviving tales of these outings, my particular favorite—and the ones where I was present, admittedly, were never among my favorites—involved one of my cousins. She was still a child when first invited to join Father on Morton's Lake. A newly arrived émigré in this country, and grateful for his kindness, she readily accepted his invitation. Today—almost six decades later and a third of a century since his death—the memory of that morning with Father has remained fresh for her.

Warning her about mosquitoes and arguing that pajamas would provide better protection than would ordinary clothing, Father convinced her to wear her night-clothes to the lake. As their adventure began, the poor girl found herself unsuitably garbed, feeling as if she were on public display, and stepping into Father's fragile-looking fishing craft, poised to set out on a seemingly stagnant lake in pursuit of fish that held not the slightest attraction. Add to that the necessity of steeling herself for the task of matching sharp hooks with live worms, and she found little impetus for either optimism or pleasure.[1] Regrettably for my cousin, there also seemed no opportunity for a reprieve. Even if the day proved a success, she figured, Father and she would be left in possession of an unsavory bounty she then—making matters even worse—would be expected to eat. As my mother's mother once commented in reference to Father's unfailing success at this sport, "There's a reason they call it a 'mess' of fish."

From her place in the boat that day, my young cousin also faced the task of fanning away the smoke of Father's cigars. He and his El Producto Favoritos were inseparable, and we all had to resign ourselves to their inescapable fetor. Unfortunately, not until after returning to shore did Father think to mention that the smoke, if allowed to hover about them in the predawn blackness, might have afforded some assistance in dispersing the advancing insects. The omission of that fact was not really neglect on his part, though. He just had an odd way of being uncompromisingly punctual yet seldom timely.

Without fail, Father would profess surprise at the woeful response with which his companions regarded these outings. What I noticed, however, was that although these fishing-mates were ruffled at the experience, they invariably emerged with nothing but love for their host. Somehow, from amid the trial of these circumstances, there would surface a recognition of something in Father that earned his comrade's affection. My cousin, like so many novice anglers before her, might resolve never to go fishing again, but she recognized nonetheless something in Father to which she was attracted for the rest of her life. The aspect of his character that I usually heard cited in such circumstances was goodness. My father had no facility at using shared interests or ambitions in forming unions. So he would simply outweigh the experience by his native undercurrent of simple goodness. Whether on a miserable predawn fishing expedition, a midnight outing for what he thought would pass for vacation sight-seeing, or amid the record-breaking pace he set each time I dragged him to a museum or chamber recital, he would emerge—inexplicably—as appealing and companionable. His associates simply had to accept—eventually, at least—that for him an event pertained only minimally to the announced objective. When fishing, for example, he applied himself zealously to the task at hand, but he really cared relatively little about the measure of the day's catch. He did care, however, about the company he kept, that is, about the person. Both parties, without fail, seemed to recognize and acknowledge that.

There was something about Father that allowed him to secure enduring friendship and affection from amidst the dark recesses of miserable experiences and unshared interests. It was his empathy. In the aftermath of one of my least successful youthful adventures, my godmother explained this quality to me perfectly: "You are a lucky boy," she said. "You broke your leg, but your father is the one who limps because of it."

That was how his empathy worked. Father was not even remotely prescient. He did not see another's discomfort nearly as quickly as one might have wished, but once he perceived it, he also experienced it. This empathy—which could so readily overwhelm his sensibilities—was for him a venue for his goodness. It marked him in a way no mere enterprise could.

Thomas Aquinas (ca. 1225–74) had an explanation for what it was about people like Father that made them so attractive as friends. Aquinas taught that goodness was inherently appealing.[2] It attracted one being to another and rendered them compatible. Moreover, goodness was made complementary when conjoined with that most fundamental of virtues: love.[3] Anselm (ca. 1033–1109) noted a similar dynamic when he observed that the right response to love is to love in return.[4] That was Father's mode of operation: He loved first and built his friendships upon that solid grounding.

As it happened, that was something of a family standard, and one that I needed to learn. The foundation of friendship was not the things or events that people shared; friendship was, instead, forged of the care of one person for the other. Rather than an option, this was proposed as ordinary means. Father's youngest brother, my Uncle Berek, was the one who taught me how expansively it was meant to be applied.

Each summer in my youth, Uncle Berek and Aunt Dora hosted me for an extended stay at their home in the Bronx. Between my rounds of museums, lectures, historical sites, and theaters, they sometimes succeeded in distracting me with lessons I needed to absorb. One of these followed upon Aunt Dora's concern about what she perceived as my lack of discernment and discretion.

Even when a young child, I was one of those people whom others— even strangers—engaged in conversation. It was just part of life for me, and I never thought of it as extraordinary. Aunt Dora, however, warned me against such encounters. She was concerned that I would fall prey to someone unsavory. Being epically without practical judgment, how- ever—"innocent" would be too kind a term, I fear—I simply accepted that my fate was, as she delineated it, that someday one of these strangers would leave me bloodied and bruised in an alley somewhere.

Because these conversations with strangers seemed so common- place to me, I never really agreed to revise my behavior. Nevertheless, Aunt Dora persisted. In response to one of her attempts, I made a pass- ing remark alluding to those encountered as "acquaintances." Suddenly, Uncle Berek entered the room, warning me never to say that again. Now Uncle Berek, who was of much the same fabric as my father, was a man of considerable gentleness. So his intensity startled both Aunt Dora and me. Nevertheless, he made his message very clear: Whether a person approached me in need, cordiality, or in circumstances less de- fined, Uncle Berek admonished, that individual should be treated as more than an "acquaintance." My uncle explained his standard this way: "Don't doubt goodness," he said. "See them each as your friend."

That counsel—"don't doubt goodness"—hit me especially hard that day. It suggested a course that I had already sensed, of course. Yet it car- ried an additional level of import because of its source. After all, I knew, the clemency and gentleness that were Uncle Berek's ordinary stance belied the troubles that marked his biography.

This uncle, his wife, and his daughter had lived through the Holocaust. After the war, they fled Poland, then snaked through much of Europe as they escaped Communists, profiteers, hunger, and indif- ference, until they found themselves seeking an ironic refuge in

Germany. Before their passage to the New World, Uncle Berek had known horrors beyond my experience, even beyond the scope of my imagination. Yet life's trials never made him lose his belief that goodness was the right response, regardless of all of the rancor and distress that—as he knew so very well—afflicted the world. Despite all that he had suffered, this man could still counsel that friendship was to be offered and realized on the foundation: "Never doubt goodness." That was a model of trust and love that he practiced and that he cared enough to recommend to an immature and unthinking nephew.

There was a real quality of goodness in that standard, the same character that Aquinas identified as so fundamentally appealing. Yet it was also just the sort of counsel that—all too often—was dismissed or at least discounted. For example, Anne Frank's famous contention that "I still believe, in spite of everything, that people are truly good at heart"[5] commonly has been portrayed as nothing more than the musings of her immaturity. After entering the camps and experiencing their horror, these arguments propose, surely she could no longer have believed in such goodness. The flaw in such latter-day appraisals is something I first perceived in my father and my uncle. They both held that one ought not to doubt goodness, seeing each person as a friend instead. Theirs was a confident affirmation of the same principle that Anselm had articulated nine centuries earlier: The right approach to a person was love. Of course, that love might not win the response Anselm—or my father or my uncle—expected in return, but a failed reply made the first person's love no less apt. The lesson was this: If you would see someone—anyone—as a friend, then they must be loved, not just companioned.

Notes

1. I suppose it should be noted that they also were probably the only people on the lake that day who were conversing in Yiddish. But because of the remotely exotic cachet lent by that distinction (at least in that setting), I suspect that they both took a certain pleasure in it.

2. Thomas Aquinas, *Summa Theologica I*, Q.5, Art. 4.

3. See Matthew 22:38.

4. See Anselm, Epistle 115.

5. Anne Frank's diary was first published in an expurgated text released by her father, Otto Frank. That edition, *Het Achterhuis,* first appeared in 1947 in Holland. After her father's death (1980), a critical edition was prepared and released, containing the full original work, plus the edited version of Anne's text, as well as Otto's truncated edition. Mirjam [sic] Pressler was appointed by the Anne Frank-Fonds to produce a definitive edition from these three separate forms. I have used the English translation (1995) of that edition: *Anne Frank, The Diary of a Young Girl: The Definitive Edition,* eds. Otto H. Frank and Mirjam Pressler, trans. Susan Massotty (London: Doubleday, 1995), 332. The quotation here was taken from Pressler's translation of Anne's diary entry of 15 July 1944.

FOUR

FRIENDSHIP AND RACE

GILBERT H. CALDWELL

Friendship evolves from and is shaped by family, childhood, school, teenage years, interests, dreams, ambition, profession, worldview, age, and racial status in the United States. In much of my writing, speaking, and living, I have addressed the last category because most of us have not yet been able to accept, explore, discuss, or act in response to the peculiar history of race in the Americas. At times as I reflect upon this, I realize that in my effort to counter the "sound of silence" on race, I have created more noise than I have wanted to in an effort to make up for the silence that I have "heard" from the not-too-friendly as well as from my friends. In the course of this chapter, this will emerge and I want to prepare the reader.

VIEWS OF FRIENDSHIP SHAPED BY BEING A GRANDFATHER
But I must begin to write about friendship in a way shaped by the fact that at age seventy I became a first-time grandfather! As I write this, my granddaughter is seventeen months old. My wife and I have had our lives, our conversations, our shopping, and much else reshaped by that little girl who resides in New Jersey. Because of the theme of this book I would say that the "friendship" that my wife and I share has taken new turns, because both of us have become sometimes foolish and different acting people due to our grandparent status. I am more patient than usual in department stores as Grace surveys the clothing in the children's sections, where she often buys something without the usual complain-

ing from me. She also is patient with me as I visit the children's sections of bookstores looking for something for Ashley.

What I found recently in the children's literature division helps launch my thoughts about friendship in this essay. Readers of this book are invited to become acquainted with *Frog and Toad Are Friends* by Arnold Lobel, an "I Can Read Book." The story titled "The Letter" is a tale that I will one day read to my granddaughter. First, let me tell you about it.

Toad was sitting on his porch and along came Frog. Frog, with the awareness and sensitivity that all authentic friends have, said, "What is the matter, Toad? You are looking sad." Toad's rejoinder was a response that articulates my feelings six days a week, that only my friend, my spouse Grace, knows about. Toad told Frog that this is his sad time of day; he was waiting for the mail, something that always made him unhappy because he never got any mail. (Unlike Toad, I get mail six days a week, but the waiting and anticipation for my mail to arrive and, most of all, the no-mail days of Sundays and holidays, I confess, makes me sad.)

Frog asked Toad, "Not ever?" (do you get mail). Toad said, "No, Never." Then Frog decided to do something that is the mark of deep, authentic, caring friendship. Frog left Toad and hurried home:

> He found a pencil and a piece of paper. He wrote on the paper. He put the paper in an envelope. On the envelope he wrote "A LETTER FOR TOAD."[1]

I believe "real friends" ask questions, listen to the answers, and then respond to the answers they have heard. "Less-than-real friends" ask the same questions, but do not pay attention to the answers they get. Authentic friendship is "hearing" not only the words, but seeking to hear the unspoken words between the words and between the lines.

Frog saw Snail and said to Snail, "Please take this letter to Toad's house and put it in his mailbox." "Sure," says the Snail. "Right away." (Now, of course, we know that any snail that says it will do something "right away" is a snail that has aspirations of being the speedy sprinter that it is not. But snails and people leave our lives, dreaming "the Impossible Dream").

Frog rushed back to Toad's house, found him in bed and said, "I think you should get up and wait for the mail some more." Toad, speaking out of his long-time depression, shaped by his never getting mail, replied, "I am tired of waiting for the mail." Frog responded, "You never know when someone may send you a letter." Frog's words did not transform Toad's depressed state. Frog kept looking out of the window hoping to see Snail bringing the letter, but there was no sign of Snail. He kept looking and looking and Toad finally said, "Frog, why do you keep looking out of the window?" Frog responded, "Because now I am waiting for the mail." Toad, of course, wondered what the reason was for his friend's state of delusion that made him now talk about waiting for the mail. (Full disclosure compels me to say that it is Caldwell, and not author Arnold Lobel, who suggests that Toad is imagining that Frog is in a delusive state).

Frog finally told Toad that he had written him a letter that said, "Dear Toad, I am glad that you are my best friend. Your best friend, Frog." Toad said, "Oh, that makes a very good letter."

The story ended with Frog and Toad sitting on the porch waiting for the mail together. "They sat there, feeling happy together," writes Lobel. They waited and waited. Four days later Snail got to Toad's house, and gave him the letter. Both Frog and Toad were very pleased. ("Four days!" I now understand the origin of the phrase "snail mail").

Frog reminds us that friendship is looking at, listening to, and doing something in response to what one has seen and heard from a friend. Then it is waiting with one's friend, in anticipation of what is to come. I think Toad would have done for Frog what Frog did for him.

BLACK AND WHITE FRIENDSHIPS

Someone has said that the number of individual friendships between blacks and whites has increased today, but racial polarization and the imbalance of resources between the two groups is on the increase. A sad commentary could be made that increased individual friendships may serve as a "cover" for the continuation of what *Sojourners* magazine once called "America's Original Sin: Racism."

I said yes to an opportunity to become senior minister of a predominantly white United Methodist Church in Colorado that had a significant presence of African Americans and Africans. My "yes" was predicated on the hope that a longtime racially integrated church was ready to discuss in depth and act vigorously upon the remaining residuals of racism. My experience in that setting caused me to coin the phrase, "It is difficult to talk about race candidly, in racially mixed company." My assessment was that longtime friendships across racial lines caused both black and white persons to back away from discussions and actions they thought would harm their friendships. Some blacks, I thought, seemed to intentionally work at protecting what they thought were the "comfort zones" of their white friends, and whites suppressed their candid comments and questions, fearful they would anger and injure their black friends.

In contrast is my longtime friendship with the co-editor of this book, Donald Messer, former president of both Dakota Wesleyan University in Mitchell, South Dakota, and Iliff School of Theology in Denver, Colorado. Don and his wife Bonnie have been friends for more than forty years. We met in Boston when I invited Don, a white native of South Dakota, to be the student minister at Union United Methodist Church in Boston, where I was the senior minister. Union, an African American congregation in Boston's South End, developed a ministry with a group of African American young men in the neighborhood who called themselves the "Grand Dukes." Don played basketball and went to municipal court with them as he served as their leader/mentor/tutor/chaplain. Today Don and I do not agree on everything, but as friends he expects I will do what I must do, just as I know he will do what he must do.

The Congressional Black Caucus is composed of the African American members of Congress. It is my understanding that, sadly, African American congresspersons who are Republican were discouraged from joining their Democratic Party colleagues. This action on their part made untrue their slogan, "We have no permanent friends, no permanent enemies, just permanent interests." How can it be that black Republicans did not share *any* of their interests?

On matters of race and other matters it is necessary to ask: Can friendship at times get in the way of justice? One of the defensive comments once heard from white southerners is that despite racial segregation, the "friendship" between whites and blacks in their region was superior to that of the north and west. But at what cost?

My long friendship with Don, and my more recent friendship with Andrew Weaver, gives me the confidence that they are not surprised when I introduce what some would say is the "race card" in our friendship writings. My view of authentic friendship is that I demean them and our friendship if I "tiptoe through the tulips" and avoid discussing race because I think their comfort zones or those of the publisher require it.

Howard Zinn has written, "There is not a country in world history in which racism has been more important, for so long a time, as in the United States. And, the problem of 'the color line,' as W. E. B. DuBois put it, is still with us." Let me share some thoughts about friendship in relation to our nation's racial history and current reality that may be applicable to all other friendships.

HOW RACIAL HISTORY AND CURRENT REALITY IMPACT FRIENDSHIPS

Racial history and current reality in the United States affect human friendships. At least four dimensions particularly deserve attention.

1. "Embedding." I borrow the term from its use to describe the presence of journalists with United States military forces fighting in Iraq. They supposedly were present in that way to give a "boots on the ground" perspective to the war in Iraq. The words of Native American Indian wisdom are probably more appropriate: "Never judge another person until you have walked in their moccasins for two weeks."

My belief about friendship across racial lines is that there must be some effort to understand the history and experience of the friend whose racial journey is different from one's own. Kermit the frog says, "It's not easy being green." Neither is it easy being black, white, brown, red, or yellow. (I recognize, as do we all, that the use of color to designate race is imprecise at best.) Pretensions of "color blindness" have a way of making my history, culture, and experience as an African American invisible to those who claim the "disease" of color blindness. If blindness to race (or gender) is a requisite for friendship, warning lights and red flags begin to surface within me.

2. Race-specific gatherings. The Million Man March, visits to African American churches, patronizing a black barbershop, participating in organizations that represent a historic response to the earlier racial apartheid of our nation—these events and actions and much more were and are important to many of us who are African American (though not all of us). White persons participate in so many white-race specific gatherings that are "normal"; they require no designation as such. Understanding the importance of homogeneous gatherings is important to friendship.

3. Justice struggles. A friend that is oblivious to the justice struggles of one's friend is a dubious friend. Frog became aware of Toad's depression because Toad never received mail. Frog acted and then waited with

Toad for his letter to arrive. Friendship deepens when we are aware of and respond to the individual and group struggles of our friends. Truly, friends "show up" in tough times as well as good times.

The superficiality of the "friendship" of southern whites for blacks became obvious when white "friends" became invisible men and women to their black friends amidst the actions of the southern civil rights movement. Christian faith and simple human kindness suggest that when persons struggle and suffer, their friends struggle and suffer with them.

4. Differing perspectives and understandings. Friendship accommodates differing perspectives and understandings. The revelation of the reality of an out-of-proportion number of poor black persons in New Orleans and elsewhere on the Gulf Coast following the devastation of Hurricane Katrina caused me to write: "The 'music' of legal racial segregation may be over, but the 'melody' lingers on."[3] Some of my friends are in radical disagreement with me as I have made this observation, but our friendship remains.

There is the same disconnect between myself and some of my friends as I support full rights and access for homosexual persons in church and society and many of my friends do not. The disconnect becomes wider as I support same gender marriage and they do not. My friendship for them compels me—rather than avoid the conversation or pretend that there are no differences between us—not to hide my perspective "under a bushel."

WAITING FOR EACH OTHER

Yvette Flunder uses the words of Paul in First Corinthians about the Lord's Supper, "So then, my brothers and sisters, when you come together to eat, wait for one another." Flunder writes,

> We can wait for each other. We can hope and believe that those who say cruel things today will say kind things tomorrow. We can wait for each other. I must bear with you and you must bear with me. We can't give up on one another, for we are all the body of Christ and we can wait for each other.[4]

In the words of the prophet Isaiah:

> They that wait upon the Lord (and each other) will renew their strength. They shall mount up with wings

like eagles, they shall run and not be weary, they shall walk and not faint. (Isa. 40:31)

This, I believe, is the essence within the friend we call Jesus. Let us follow him, as we are friends of Jesus and of each other! Yes, friendship and race in the United States continue to require us to wait for each other.

Notes

1. Arnold Lobel, *Frog and Toad Are Friends* (New York: Harper-Collins, 1970).

2. Howard Zinn, *A People's History of the United States, 1491–Present* (New York: Perennial Classic/HarpersCollins, 1980), 23.

3. Gilbert H. Caldwell, Note 4. Gilbert H. Caldwell, *What Mean These Stones? Lessons of Hurrican Katrina, 9/11, the Million Man March, the Millions More Movement* (iUniverse, 2005).

4. Yvette Flunder, *Where the Edge Gathers* (Cleveland: Pilgrim Press, 2005), 120.

FIVE

HE LIVES ON DEATH ROW
An Imprisoned Friend

KENNETH L. CARDER

What began as an interview by a high school newspaper reporter became an enduring and transforming friendship. As the associate editor of her high school newspaper, our daughter, Sheri, set out to write a feature article on the death penalty. In addition to a literature search, Sheri chose to interview an inmate on death row. Since I had been involved in prison ministries over the years, I knew officials who could make such an interview possible.

After several weeks of navigating the bureaucratic maze of the Tennessee State Corrections system, Sheri and I were cleared to visit William (Bill) Groseclose. Bill's trustworthiness as a prisoner for the last four years and the ease with which he interacted with inmates, guards, and visitors made him a "safe" interviewee.

On an October day in 1982, Sheri and I drove the 175 miles from Knoxville, Tennessee, to Nashville for our first visit with Bill. Since I had visited jails and prisons for fifteen years, I tried to prepare my sixteen-year-old daughter to enter the bleak, dangerous, and insecure world behind prison bars.

The Tennessee State Penitentiary was one of the worst in the nation. A federal lawsuit had been filed charging that the prison's conditions amounted to "cruel and unusual punishment." The state was under court order to improve the conditions of the old fortresslike facility that had been built in 1898. Behind the high stone walls with towers sheltering heavily armed guards lived two thousand inmates, almost double its capacity.

After receiving our passes and undergoing our pat-down searches, Sheri and I made our way through six iron gates before reaching the interior prison yard. Men dressed in prison uniforms roamed the area, some huddled in small groups, others sitting idly against the stone wall. Lining the yard were fortresslike stone buildings housing inmates who were not permitted to mingle with the general prison population.

As we made our way through the yard toward the concrete building called Unit Six, located behind the heavily guarded and fortified walls, we felt the stares of inmates and the watchful eyes of heavily armed guards. "Cat calls" and whistles came from the barred windows of the adjacent cells as our red-haired daughter and I made our way to "death row."

After entering the heavy steel entrance to Unit Six, we were escorted into a dimly lit concrete-walled room with no window. A steel table and six chairs, plus a wall-mounted blackboard, comprised the furnishings. The door locked behind us. This was the visitation room for those able to have face-to-face visits and a classroom for those permitted to participate in the limited educational activities. As Sheri and I waited nervously for Bill to be escorted into the visitation room, we spotted one of the nation's most infamous inmates, James Earl Ray, mopping the floor in the adjacent entrance way. On the chalkboard hanging on the classroom bars was one inmate's image of Jesus. Underneath the etching were these words, "He lives on death row."

The steel door to the visiting area opened and Bill was escorted handcuffed into the room. He greeted us with a bright smile and a joyful "Hello, you must be Sheri and Reverend Carder." The guard removed the cuffs. We smilingly shook hands and took our seats around the metal table anchored to the floor. The guard moved to one side, but he remained within sight and hearing throughout the conversation.

Bill had introduced himself in a series of letters prior to our visit. He was born in 1948 in Southwestern Virginia and he was the father of four children. He had been in the U.S. Navy and was serving as a recruiter when he was charged in 1977 with having his wife murdered. He was convicted and sentenced to death in 1978. Although we did not discuss his case, he was appealing his conviction.

For two hours on that initial visit, Bill openly shared is views on topics ranging from his own family background to his perspective on the death penalty. The conversation was mixed with laughter and serious reflection. It was immediately evident that Bill was exceptionally smart, articulate, well-read, and informed on many issues. He described the conditions under which he and his fellow inmates lived, including daily exposure to rats, roaches, suffocating heat in summer, and chilling cold in winter. He talked freely of the possibility of his making the trip to the chamber at the end of his hallway that housed "Ole Smokey," the name prisoners had given to the electric chair.

I asked, "Bill, given the circumstances under which you live, how do you maintain hope and a positive spirit?" He responded, "The philosophers had it right. Some things in life are so tragic that you have to cry. Others are so comical, you have to laugh. But most things are a mixture of tragedy and comedy. In those, you have a choice. You can choose to laugh or cry. When I have a choice, I choose to laugh." Pointing to the drawing on the chalkboard, he added, "That helps, too. We aren't alone here."

That first visit was followed by countless letters and regular visits over subsequent years. The friendship deepened and expanded to include the entire family. Bill's letters to Sheri were filled with advice and encouragement as she graduated from high school and entered college. He became what Sheri described later as "a beloved uncle" and friend. We were the beneficiaries of his artistic and craft talents as his paintings decorated our home.

Bill lived awaiting death for twenty years. Multiple appeals were filed and dismissed. Execution dates were set and postponed. On one occasion, he came within three days of being executed. Conditions within the prison itself improved, partly as the result of a petition Bill filed in federal court on behalf of the inmates on death row. The federal judge, who made an unannounced visit to death row, found the prison in violation of the Constitutional protection against cruel and unusual punishment. A new prison was built.

Bill's behavior and skills earned him a "trustee" position and he was assigned to work in the office on death row. He taught GED classes, painting, and Bible courses to other inmates; and he continued his own learning by taking college-level correspondence courses in a variety of subjects, including Bible and theology.

My visits with Bill included levity and gravity. We knew the comic and the tragic, laughter and tears. Neither title nor position mattered to

Bill. He never called me "Reverend" after that first introductory visit. I was always "Ken" or "my friend." His guilt or innocence ceased to be a judgment I needed to make. His confinement and prospective execution grieved me deeply. Our conversations easily moved from shared family stories to theological discussions, from political commentary to speculating on upcoming sports events. He was always able to detect pretense and seemed to have an intuitive empathy. When he detected an element of posturing in me or others, he would laughingly dismantle it with "Now, you can't con a con."

A turning point in our friendship was my election to the episcopacy in 1992. I was serving as the pastor of Church Street United Methodist Church in Knoxville. Bill and I had by then been friends for ten years. We corresponded regularly and I made occasional trips to Nashville to visit him, though the schedule and limited visiting hours made the visits difficult and more infrequent than we preferred. He knew that I was being considered for the episcopacy and he had shared with a mutual friend that he hoped I would be elected.

Late in the afternoon of the day in July 1992 on which my election was announced in the morning, a call came to our home at Lake Junaluska, North Carolina. Upon answering the phone, my wife, Linda, called to me, "It's Bill!" "Bill who?" I asked. "Bill Groseclose," she responded almost in tears. I went to the phone and the first words I heard were, "Finally, an American election that turns out right. I knew this was going to happen."

"How did you know? How are you making this call?" I asked. He told me that our associate pastor had called and he happened to be in the office working at the time. "But who gave you permission to call me, and you didn't call collect this time." "That's another story and I will tell you later" he replied. He congratulated me and told me how thankful he was "that the church had the good sense to elect you. Now if they will have the sense to assign you to Nashville!"

I was assigned to Nashville, and our home was just two miles from the Tennessee State Prison! Bill and I were neighbors! Frequent visits became possible. Telephone calls, though limited by prison rules, happened more often. Though my title changed and my first name was customarily replaced by "Bishop," I remained "Ken" to Bill.

As had been the case over the years, Bill never asked or even hinted that I intervene on his behalf. Unlike so many who seemed to want something from "the bishop," Bill never wanted anything from me but the friendship we had shared for ten years. With him I could be myself as I confronted life's comedy and tragedy. My visits with Bill persistently reminded me amid the challenges and conflicts, inspirations and disappointments of the episcopacy that I had choices whether to laugh or cry and that the One who "lives on death row" will never leave me alone. Bill's authenticity and unconditional acceptance persistently challenged my temptations to hide personal vulnerability behind the episcopal office and to be seduced by public pomp and praise.

I learned in my first visit with Bill after moving to Nashville in September 1992 how he was able to make the telephone call in July. The captain on duty in the office that day owed a special debt to Bill. When a riot had broken out on death row in the old prison facility approximately eight years previously, the current captain had been taken hostage by the rioting inmates. Bill was not among the rioters but he was in the area where the violence was taking place. He intervened on behalf of the guards and helped to avoid further violence. The captain credits Bill with saving his life. Therefore, when my colleague called the prison and they put him through to death row, he gave the captain the message of my election. When he relayed the news to Bill, he asked, "Would you like to call him?"

During the ensuing seven years, I was able to visit Bill about twice per month. His teaching and office work continued. Although confined to death row, he had more freedom than most of the men who shared the unit. He was trusted by prison officials and inmates. He was considered the "unofficial chaplain" of death row as well as an expert "jail house lawyer." Since my visits took place during regular visiting times for families and friends, the room was usually filled with visitors. Bill knew them all! Most of the men in the unit were much younger than Bill and some of them looked to him as a father figure or older brother, roles he seemed to fill willingly and naturally.

Bill's twenty-year attempt to get a new trial finally materialized when a Court of Appeals ruled in 1998 that several errors had been made in his original trial. He was transferred from death row to the Memphis jail in preparation for a new trial scheduled for February 1999. Two young brother/sister attorneys agreed to defend Bill. They contacted Bill's acquaintances, including Sheri and me, and we provided information recounting our relationship with him over the previous sixteen years.

I visited him in the Memphis jail where he was confined to a small cell twenty-three hours each day. He lacked the warm relationships and work opportunities that had characterized his life on death row. He now shared a crowded cell with several other prisoners and the noise was loud and continuous. Face-to-face visits were forbidden and we were separated by a heavy steel door with a small translucent window. A crackling telephone made conversation nearly impossible.

The case received extensive media attention. Bill became a symbol of the death penalty controversy. Current and aspiring politicians used Bill's case to advance their ambitions. Death penalty advocates bemoaned the slowness of the state in executing death row inmates and attributed the delay to "liberal judges" who were "soft on crime." A petition calling for the impeachment of a federal judge who had ruled in Bill's and other cases was circulated. "Letters to the Editor" regarding the death penalty appeared almost daily in newspapers across the state as Bill's trial date approached.

Since Sheri and I had not known Bill prior to his original trial and sentencing, we had no contribution to make in the evidentiary phase of the trial. The attorneys indicated that if a guilty verdict was returned, we would be called to testify during the sentencing phase. With anxiety and dread, we received daily updates of the trial from the news reports as well as calls from a friend who attended the proceedings.

After several days of testimony and arguments, the case went to the jury and our anxiety increased. Finally, the news came. Guilty of first degree murder! The attorneys requested that Sheri and I come to Memphis and testify in an attempt to spare Bill another death sentence. Sheri drove to Nashville from her home in Knoxville. After a night of little sleep and much grief, we left early for the three-hour trip to Memphis. Much of the drive was in silence as we felt the heaviness of what awaited us and rehearsed our testimony in our minds.

We arrived in the courtroom for the start of the testimony. Bill was seated at the defendant's table with his attorneys and codefendant. We took seats behind him and beside his older cousin, who had helped to raise him. She had been present throughout the trial. Across the aisle sat several family members of the victim, including Bill's son, who was about the age of Sheri. Bill did not turn toward us but stared without emotion toward the presiding judge. We listened intently to the prosecuting attorney as he portrayed Bill as a ruthless murderer who deserved no mercy.

Following the testimony of Bill's cousin, Sheri was called to the stand. She had sat nervously between me and her mother, often taking our hands and gently squeezing. She carried to the witness stand a box that contained all the letters she had received from Bill over the last sixteen years. She was nervous but poised as Bill's attorney questioned her about her friendship with Bill. The attorney asked, "How would you describe your relationship with him?" Sheri responded, "He is like an adopted uncle. He has given me encouragement and advice. I have learned a lot from him."

When asked what she had learned, she replied, "You can't ultimately judge people by stereotypes. You have to get to know them as people, and people on death row are people, too." She shared that the only thing Bill ever asked her for was the color of her room. He wanted his paintings for her to match her room's decor. Sheri gave a glimpse of Bill's humor by recounting that he had her mom and dad put rice in her car at her wedding with a note, "I just wanted to let you know I was here. Sorry I couldn't stay for the reception, Bill."

It was now my turn to take the stand. I recounted many experiences with Bill, including his call when I was elected a bishop. Jurors laughed when I reported his comment, "Finally an American election that turned out right." I emphasized the contribution he had made to our family and the other prisoners who had benefited from his teaching and counsel. When asked if he had value to me, I declared, "He certainly does and he has value to God." The prosecutor rose in objection to my reference to God. The judge sustained the objection. The irony was that the court administered the oath to me in the name of God, but I could make no reference to God in my testimony. But the objection did not remove the statement from the hearing of the jurors.

Other witnesses for Bill included the former warden and other correctional officers, including the captain who had permitted him to make the phone call to me in 1992. They described him as a model prisoner who was like a staff member. Two men who shared death row with him testified to Bill's ministry to them. Both had received their GEDs under his tutorage and they testified that their lives had been "turned around" by their friendship with Bill. They both shared how Bill lifted their morale, especially on holidays when he decorated the cellblock. One shared the story of Bill painting pictures of animals and "Smurfs," contributing them anonymously to the children as Christmas gifts.

Following summation by the attorneys and instructions from the judge, the jury retired to consider the sentencing. We waited throughout the day, receiving angry stares from the prosecuting attorneys and family members. News media members present interacted jovially with those seeking Bill's execution and avoided contact with us.

Late in the afternoon, the red light flashed, indicating the jury had reached a decision. We filed into the courtroom and took our seats behind Bill. Sheri, my wife, Linda, Bill's cousin, and I joined hands as the verdict was handed to the judge. Tears flowed as the sentence was read, "Life in prison." Bill turned toward us and puzzlingly smiled. He had said before the trial that if he was not acquitted he wanted to be returned to death row. His life had been spared but he was not rejoicing. Death row had become home and familiar. Further, he feared that legal recourse would cease if he received a life sentence.

The attorneys indicated that the testimony by Sheri and me was critical in saving Bill from execution. Apparently the friendship we shared over sixteen years was seen as evidence of Bill's humanity and his value to society. Our brief appearance on his behalf in a Memphis courtroom does not compare with the contribution that Bill has made to our lives.

Bill was returned to Nashville and placed in the general population. For the first time in twenty-one years, he was able to lie in the grass on the prison grounds. Once again he could hear the birds and look for a four-leaf clover. He viewed rabbits playing outside the prison fence and kept watch over a family of sparrows nestled in a nearby tree.

But his newfound hope was soon tested. He was mysteriously reclassified and transferred to another facility located in a remote area of West Tennessee. His attorneys suspect that political pressure was applied to the Department of Correction to make conditions as harsh as possible. His new location made visits by his cousin impossible and difficult for his friends.

I made the three-hour trip to the rural community where Bill is now housed one time before I was transferred from Nashville to Jackson, Mississippi, in September 2000. He was discouraged but still hopeful. The circumstances were tragic but he still found humor. He refused to permit his mind to be imprisoned. He had often remarked, "They've got my body, but they can't have my mind." We parted with an embrace and a promise of continued friendship.

Our physical contacts have diminished with changes in health, distance, and circumstances. But the friendship continues and Bill's influence grows even stronger with reflection on his remarkable life amid the most tragic of events and circumstances. Through our friendship, I have come to deeper conviction of the profound reality portrayed by the etching we first saw on the chalkboard in that foreboding cell almost twenty-five years ago, "He lives on death row."

SIX

LIVING BY GOD'S GRACE
Agnes, Anna, and Agnes

MUSA W. DUBE

n my native language of Setswana, spoken in Botswana, Africa, a friend is referred to as *tsala* and friendship is *botsala*. Friends are *ditsala*. The noun *tsala* seems to be derived from the verb *tsala*, which means giving birth (the difference is in intonation). Consequently, *tsala* is the root word of many words that refer to blood relations. For example, the reflexive word *tsalana* means to be related to one another or relatives; *ntsalake* means cousin, *botsalano* means to be in a relationship, which may or may not be a blood relationship. Since *tsala* as a verb means "to give birth," friendship is somewhat a process of birthing one another—giving life and refreshing each other.

THOSE WHO PICK EACH OTHER'S TEETH

This subtle connotation is perhaps hinted in another Setswana phrase that describes a friend as *kala yame*, literally meaning my branch, as in a tree. Here a friend is described as a natural extension and part of oneself, hence, my branch. Friendship is thus a process of branching into each other, becoming part of one another. Both the noun *tsala* and the phrase *kala yame* underline closeness in the relationship of friendship, to the extent that while it is not biological, it is described in biological terms.

This closeness of friendship is specifically captured in a Setswana saying that describes friends as *ba ba ntshanang se seinong*, literally

44

"those who pick each other's teeth!" No doubt, picking one's teeth is a private practice, for obvious reasons. To describe friends as "those who pick each other's teeth" is to underline the closeness of friendship: with a friend one can be free and nothing needs to be hidden or is too hideous or embarrassing to be revealed. The fact that the word for a friend, *tsala*, is the root word that defines all relationships perhaps highlights that friendship is at the center of all relationships. Without some element of friendship even blood relationships cannot work.

"BIRTHING" FRIENDSHIP

I have been truly blessed with many friends along the journey of life. Different friends, in various places and at different times, have come to interweave their journeys with mine. One thing I have discovered is that I do not decide who will be my friend. I only come to know that I have a friend when I already have one—one who has begun to birth me—when that person has become a natural extension of me, *kala yame*. When such an event occurs then I have experienced a miracle of resurrection. I am renewed and energized to walk the walk of life, to face life not only as a chore but as joy as well.

Friends punctuate life with laughter, fun, affirmation, acceptance, love, care, and compassion. In front of friends you become whole: accepted for what you are, advised where you need it, and left alone to make choices and decisions that you need to make, but assured company in whatever comes your way. In friendship one can come to realize one of the rare experiences of appearing perfect even in one's weakness. In friendship one's self esteem is thus boosted and one's creative lights are lit. Friendship makes one ready to confront oneself and to see what one can be without fear.

FRIENDS AS ROSES AND ANGELS

Friendship certainly makes me understand that I am not alone, that I am accompanied, that I am loved. I thus regard friends as roses and angels that come along the road of life and make the journey of life more enjoyable and bearable. They are roses since they punctuate life with beauty and love. They help me appreciate the beauty of life. They make me see the flowers. They encourage me to stop and smell the roses. They make me see myself and love myself. They help me know love and give love. Indeed, life without friends would have less sparkle.

No doubt one makes friends where one lives, works, and socially interacts; that is, friends punctuate one's life along the places where one's journey of life meanders. My friends have thus come from clubs, workplaces, towns and cities of abode. Because I grew up active in the Student Christian Movement, Scripture Union, Christian Union, church, and ecumenical movements, most of my friends have been drawn from these social interactions. From my high school days there were Grace Paul, Anna Mmolawa-Motsewabeng, Motshidisi Pansiri-Ditshotlo, Agnes Mokobi-Bulawa, and Rose Ndzinge. During college I was lucky enough to be in the same town with Anna, Agnes, and Rose. During postgraduate study in foreign countries there was Sally, Nicole Wilkinson-Duran, and Leticia Guardiola-Saenz. In my workplaces (University of Botswana, World Council of Churches, and Scripps College), I journeyed with Bagele Chilisa, Nyambura Njoroge, Malebogo Kgalemang, Althea Spencer Miller, and Kathleen O'Brien Wicker.

Although one of my friends, Rosinah Baiphetlhi, has passed on and I have lost physical contact with others, they nevertheless have not lost their place in my heart and the trail of my life. All my friends of the past and present are shining stars. They remain among the many stars that sparkle in the sky of my life. The memory of our time continues to brighten and sustain me. Each friend is thus like a precious pearl in the beads of my life history. My friends are also angels, for they sustain me in times when the valleys of life are too deep to cross, the cliffs and the mountains too steep to climb. They know how to clasp my hand in theirs and to say, "Come with me; I will walk with you. You will make it." When my eyes are blinded by salty tears of the pain of life, they become my sight until such a time that my vision has cleared. When my feet are too weary with the walk of life they lend me a shoulder to lean on; when I become too sad or too serious, they remind me how to smile. When I say, "But where is God? " their love shows me God, for God is love.

SHINING STARS SPARKLING IN THE SKY OF MY LIFE

Anna, my "twin." Of the above mentioned stars, I want briefly to talk about Anna Mmolawa-Motsewabeng, Agnes Mokobi-Bulawa, and Agnes Tafa Dube, my mother and my friend. Anna was a tiny girl who, surprisingly, now a parent of three and in her forties, still remains the same. We had such a great friendship that we called each other twins.

I really cannot exactly remember where and when I met Anna. Yet it was in our high school days and our involvement in the Student Christian Movement that our paths first crossed. Then we happened to be in the same church. We were into singing in church and had a duet that sang great songs such as "a new year is born, a new day is come" and "I am going where the roses never fade." Later in my college days, Rose Ndzinge joined our duet and we became a trio called the Redeemed Sisters. We became a hit in the church and ecumenical youth movements such as Christian Union, Action Group, and the Jesus Generation Movement. When Rose graduated early and left college, Anna and I and joined the interdenominational group Hope for Today and continued with our gospel singing. But to take the clock back to high school days, Anna went to school in a different town. Consequently we wrote each other many letters. Anna was such a great writer that I used to carry her letters around, but unfortunately I lost the whole bunch of them. Anna finished high school a year earlier than me. Every weekend she would come visit me at my high school, where I was boarding. One day the matron said to her, "You visit quite frequently, why don't you just move to this school!" When we went for our tertiary education, Anna went to a nursing college and I went to the University of Botswana. But Anna was always at the University of Botswana visiting me and Agnes. Many people just assumed she was a student there.

Agnes, my roommate. I also met Agnes Mokobi-Bulawa during our high school days and through our active involvement in the Student Christian Movement. She was also in a different town and school than me. But we would meet during Student Christian Movement camp meetings and hand-over ceremonies. Just after we finished high school and were waiting to start the fall semester at the University of Botswana (UB), I bumped into Agnes in a shopping complex in Francistown. We stopped and talked and then she went her way. I called her back and said, "Would you mind being my roommate at UB?" She said no. That marked the beginning of a long and profound friendship. We were roommates for three years and, during the final year, when each of us got a single room, we ensured that our rooms were next to each other.

During these three years we walked around together, went to parties, shopping, church, and Christian fellowship meetings. We were in the habit of talking long into the night when the lights were off until

I was so sleepy I could not construct a coherent sentence. Normally when the semester ended we evaluated our relationship and prayed together over issues that hurt and renewed our friendship. We had a lot of fun and found much to laugh about. During our UB days we never locked our room, since we said we had drawn the blood line of Jesus against all thieves—it worked for four good years! Our room thus became the coffee room, where people came in for tea and coffee, even when we were not there. Uncle Oats Wamana, one of the brothers in Christian Union, said in our room was where real fellowship among Christians happened.

Agnes and I became so close that people just assumed that we also discussed and planned when and whom to date, when to get pregnant and become mothers. Although it was not necessarily true, it looked like it and it was hard to convince people otherwise. Anna visited us a lot and spent many days and nights with us in our room. When both Agnes and Anna got married it was obvious that I would be the maid of honor, or the best lady, and I was. We have continued to journey together ever since those school and college days.

Along the road of life, as we journey we have not only had laughter and joy; we have also had our share of tears, losing siblings, children, and parents. Early last year when I lost my mother, Agnes and Anna came to the funeral. Later in the year, we stood together at the unveiling of the tombstone singing, "When it hurts, oh why don't you give it to Jesus." And this brings me to my mother, whom I regarded as a close friend.

Agnes, my mother. My mother, Agnes Tafa Dube, was a beautiful woman, physically and spiritually. She was not only a mother to me. She was also my friend and my spiritual mother, who taught me faith in God. My life and hers were stories of "living by grace," which is the name that she gave to me, forty-one years ago, when I was born.

I was born at home because at that time my mother was a member of a church that did not allow its members to go to the hospital. After I was delivered, the placenta remained in my mother's womb for another week. My mother was at the point of death when my grandmother, who was a *sangoma*, a traditional spirit medium and healer, arrived. She went to dig a herb from the bush, boiled it, and gave it to my mother to drink. The placenta came out immediately thereafter. Having survived death, my mother said that she "lived by the grace of God."

In the southern African way of naming, which includes recalling the event/s surrounding birth, I was named accordingly as "*musa we nkosi*," the grace of God. My name was testimony to my mother's gratefulness to God for having been granted a chance to remain alive. My first lesson of faith was ingrained in my given name. "By the grace of the God" is instrumental, yet *musa* (grace) *we* (of) *nkosi* (God) without "by" easily reads from a possessive/genitive case as "Musa/grace of God." Although historically I knew the name spoke of what God did for us (my mother and me), I could not get away from the fact that without the wider context, the name carried and sounded as a genitive/possessive case, so that it was "grace of God" rather than "by the grace of God." The name thus carries both the instrumental and genitive sense to me—living by the grace of God and living for the grace of God. The genitive angle of my name—that I am grace, who belongs to God—has often made me feel that my mother dedicated me to God at birth. Many people have encouraged me to get ordained in the church or offered to ordain me, but I have felt satisfied with the consecration that occurred when my mother named me Musa-we-nkosi at birth.

I learned this story of my name quite early because when I was small my father was fond of calling me Manto, a short form of *Mantombazana*, meaning "girls." This was because I was the fifth girl among the seven siblings.

But suddenly as I grew up I realized that I was no longer called Manto, but Musa. One day when my mother was sitting quietly under a tree, I said to her, "Can I ask you a question?" When she agreed, I said, "I remember that I used to be called Manto, but now everybody calls me Musa. Why this change?" My mother told me the story of my birth and that she got worried when the name Manto became popular since she did not want the name Musa to disappear due to its significance. Consequently, she made it a point to start using my given name until everybody got used to calling me Musa. She wanted to remember God's saving grace. But it was not only she who was grateful to God for being alive, I also was thankful to God for having saved her for me, for having allowed my mother to live so that I grew up with a mother rather than as an orphan.

In May 2005, when my mother died, I realized how blessed we were for God's prevailing grace that covered us for four decades of being together. It hurt a lot to lose my mother. I felt so lost. I did not know how to live in a world where she was not in existence. Yet this profound sense of loss also brought home to me how blessed I had been to have her as my mother and my friend for four decades. I could not forget that she and I had in fact had forty-one years of living by grace.

The story of my mother and me was not only written in our memories and names, it was also written in the thorns that remained chiseled in her body after my birth. My mother's health was never whole. Thereafter, she always remembered my birth as the point when she almost died, as a time where she was granted grace to live, and as a moment where she never fully recovered her health but rather lived in perpetual physical suffering. I could not separate myself from either her gratefulness or her suffering. I came to see in her face, literally, the face of Christ crucified. But God's grace also reminded me of the resurrection power in our lives. Consequently, we developed a very special and deep bond. I learned how to be thankful, how to celebrate every moment with her, how to care, how to be compassionate. We shared prayer, we shared songs. On summer evenings, after eating we would sing hymns of thanksgiving and praise—watching the intense skies of a billion stars at our farm home.

As I grew up, I was determined to do all I could do in my power to make my mother happy and healthy. Although I could not achieve my goal, in the process I somehow became for her the actualization of God's grace in her life—the reminder that God cares and loves us. Later on I wanted to be a nurse, but my first boyfriend dissuaded me, saying he would not wish to have a wife who worked during the night! But growing up with my mother and my story, getting close to those who are suffering and giving care and compassion seemed to come naturally to me. How I got intricately involved with the HIV/AIDS struggle in Africa for the World Council of Churches is rooted in the story of living by grace and the challenge to give grace as well.

LOVING BRANCHES OF ONE ANOTHER: MY SON AND ME

I am now a mother of a boy of eighteen years, Aluta. One of our quarrels is that he says I am his friend and I have to underline, "I am your mother." And then he says, "But you are also my friend; I tell you everything." When my mother passed on, I was in California. Aluta sent me an e-mail saying, "I am sorry, Mama. There is no love like the love from your queeny. I want you to know that you are the greatest mom of all time and I will always love you. Happy Mother's Day! I want you know that you are appreciated and cared for. I am sorry you had to lose your mom like that. She was an angel because she made you, Mama. You are my star."

This is my story of friends and friendship, *ditsala*, those who birth us, biologically, spiritually, and otherwise. Friends grow in us and we grow in them, becoming branches of one another, *kala yame*.

SEVEN

WON'T YOU BE MY NEIGHBOR?

VINCE ISNER

"He asked Jesus, 'And who is my neighbor?'" (Luke 10:29b). Picture stepping into a space as comfortable as a favorite pair of shoes, as inviting as a familiar lullaby, as warm as a sweater knit lovingly just for you.

That is almost, though not quite, what it was like to meet Fred Rogers for the first time.

I was twenty-one, recently graduated with a degree in music, and had my heart set on serving children and their families through television. My wife had suggested that I call Mister Rogers and try to meet with him to discuss the world of children's television before embarking on a graduate program. Having grown up in Pittsburgh, where Fred Rogers lived and worked, she knew all about Mister Rogers, from his early days on the local daily program *Children's Corner* to his rise as America's "television neighbor." I knew only vaguely of *Mister Rogers' Neighborhood* and even less about the man himself.

Thirty seconds—no—ten seconds into the conversation, I knew I had met someone very special. In his now famous calm, inviting manner, he asked about my interest in children (I had never taught a single day) and about my interest in television (I had never set foot inside a studio). Fred listened to my every word with an intensity I had not anticipated. In turn, I wanted to know everything about his decision to serve children, his interest in puppets, music, and drama, and his sense of calling. He answered with a depth that revealed a formidable command of philosophy, psychology, and theology as well. Clearly this man was at home with himself and with regions of the human spirit that few have dared to tread. "I think I must be an emotional archeologist," he would tell me years later, "I am so interested in the roots of human relationships."

I quickly learned that for Fred Rogers, children's television was far more about children than television and that "the neighborhood," as he called it, was an intentional means of sharing deep and abiding truths about what it means to be in community with one another.

We became fast friends and Fred became my graduate advisor. Throughout my graduate work Fred assigned many books, we scheduled many visits, and I learned many lessons. I soon learned that Rogers was a highly disciplined man who swam daily, prayed ceaselessly, read constantly, laughed easily (though not too much), and, quiet though he was, never shied away from life's harsher realities, especially when he could envision a way to help.

However, the most important lessons I learned from Fred Rogers were not found in the books he assigned, nor in the letters he wrote (though I cherish every one for their warmth and wisdom), but rather by observing Fred interact with those with whom he came into contact. If anyone knew what it meant to be a neighbor in the biblical sense, it was Fred Rogers.

Walking about with Mister Rogers in his neighborhood was simply life-changing. From a visit over lunch in my graduate school days in the late 1970s to a warm afternoon a few years before Fred's death in 2003, and all the times in between, Fred Rogers embodied kindness and grace.

"Would you mind if someone joins us for lunch today?" Fred asked at that late '70s Friday lunchtime meeting, "I think you will like Jack." I was delighted to meet anyone who was a friend of Fred Rogers.

We left the studio, drove downtown, and walked a couple of blocks. Then, instead of turning into the restaurant, Fred led me into the lobby of the old Pittsburgh YMCA, onto a musty elevator, and finally up to the seventh floor, where we walked down a dark, seedy hallway to a brown painted door. Knocking, he said, "Jack, it's Fred and Vince." Just fifteen minutes earlier we had been standing in the set of the Neighborhood of Make-believe. Now there we were, Fred in his crisp slacks, white shirt, bow tie, and jacket, announcing our presence from the hallway of a flophouse in the middle of downtown Pittsburgh.

The door opened and, to my astonishment, there stood a muscled, bearded, long-haired roughneck in a black t-shirt and jeans with a gaze that made me think we had knocked on the wrong door. However his expression quickly turned to a smile and he said, "Fred! Hey, man, good to see you. Come in." We stepped inside a decidedly "uninviting" room. (Trust me, the Village People notwithstanding, it is *not* fun to live at the YMCA!) There was, however, one homey touch—a picture of a smiling gold-sweatered Mister Rogers pinned to the wall next to the door.

We were in the right room after all.

At the restaurant I learned that Jack was my age, though an abusive childhood, a brutal adolescence, and some bad decisions resulting in a short incarceration had left him hardened and aged. Jack explained that he had met Mister Rogers in prison at the playroom that Fred had helped to create (to give inmates a comfortable place to visit their children) and where Rogers had noticed his delight and ease with youngsters. I learned that Fred had taken an interest in Jack, and, following Jack's release, was helping him get on his feet again. Jack, in turn, was teaching Mister Rogers a thing or two about life on the other side of the tracks. And the conversation—well, it was fascinating, and went something like this:

> JACK: "Whatcha working on for the show, Fred?"
>
> FRED: "We are doing a week of programs on the theme of going away and coming back. It's very important for children to understand that, you know. By the way, Jack, did you talk with your parole officer this week?"
>
> JACK: "Yeah, but he says I can't do the parking meter job since I have a record. And, yea, I know a thing or two about parents going away and *not* coming back."
>
> FRED: "Well, you know I am certainly interested in your story."

Witnessing such an unlikely exchange between two vastly different yet obviously trusted friends, Fred and Jack taught me a vital lesson that day. I learned that the human heart is a vast and holy space, and it takes great courage to stand at its door and knock.

It also takes great courage to open it.

Many years and nearly twenty-five years of visits later, I met Fred, again for lunch. This time we walked to a neighborhood café, passing through a residential area. As we walked I glanced down and noticed a blue baby pacifier on the sidewalk. I stepped over it and kept going.

Fred noticed it and stopped. Picking it up, he said to me, "Someone has lost something very important." And before I could nod in agreement, he was bolting up the steps of the nearest house, again, knocking on a door.

A young woman answered and smiled immediately, "Mister Rogers—what a surprise!" Fred showed her the pacifier, "Do you have any idea whose this may be?" The woman answered, "Yes, that's my son's." "Oh, good," Fred smiled, handing her the pacifier, "I thought there might be someone who would really miss it."

Twenty-five years of visits, and here, to my delight, was another life lesson: The human heart is indeed a vast and holy space, worthy of touching and being touched by those whose faces we may never see.

One day I asked Fred what it was like to appear on stage with the president of the United States. He shared a few general impressions, then became very quiet and said, "You know, Vince, the longer I live the more I realize that life's most important moments are rarely in the spotlight. I think that the really important dramas almost always happen in the wings, where few people notice. It may be a quiet moment in which a person forgives another and helps create a nourishing space for that person—or perhaps just a time when we are there for someone who needs us—those are the things that matter most."

I thought of how he was there for a brief moment for a baby who had lost something very important. I recalled how he was there for Jack—not just for a lunchtime, but for a lifetime. Fred Rogers wrote to Jack, visited with him whenever Jack was in town, and called him religiously the first Saturday of every month until the day Fred died.

If I have learned anything at all from walking about in Mister Rogers' "real" neighborhood, it is this—being a good neighbor certainly is not dependent upon who our neighbor is, and it is not necessarily about what we decide to *do* to be a good neighbor. Rather it is more about deciding the kind of neighbor we want to *be*—and then being that person no matter what.

The Hebrew word for salvation is *shu-a* (as in Joshua, which means "he who saves"). Salvation does not mean to pluck from damnation or to correct some wrong thinking. Salvation means to create a space for—to prepare a place for.

So thank you, dear friend, for teaching me through our walks, our talks, and those extraordinary times out of the spotlight, what it means to be a good neighbor. I know now that the human heart can be a vast and holy space. Though it beats quietly and is rarely at center stage, it is nevertheless the very neighborhood in which all true salvation happens, both to the one who knocks and to the one who answers.

EIGHT

THE "HOLY FRIENDS" OF A GLOBAL JOURNALIST

KATHLEEN LACAMERA

As a global journalist, there are so many people who have helped sustain and nurture me in my faith journey: people who have inspired me, guided me, fought for me, cared for me, forgiven me. Let me introduce you to four very special "holy friends."

GARLINDA BURTON IN THE UNITED STATES

I first met Garlinda Burton in 1985 when she was a reporter for the United Methodist Church's national news service. At the ripe old age of twenty-eight, this funny, smart, fearless, and welcoming woman seemed to know *everyone* in the denomination. I was in total awe of her. More than two decades later, I still am.

Back then I was a nervous, beginner television reporter/producer drafted out of the ranks of ordained parish ministry to lend my youth, gender, and theological training to a new television series. It was called *Catch the Spirit* and its creators (including the larger-than-life television producer, the late Rev. Bruno Caliandro) were aiming to broadcast in-spiring faith stories about United Methodists to television audiences across the United States. I had to learn a lot and fast.

When on a Friday afternoon I needed to find an African bishop to explain the delicate political/social situation affecting the church in sub-Saharan Africa, Garlinda could tell me where and how to find one. When I had to get through to a United Methodist U.S. senator for a comment on a key piece of social legislation, Garlinda knew how to by-pass the aides and assistants and get straight to the senator. When I wanted a special choir for a Christmas show or a mime artist for a creative worship segment or a world-class church historian for discussion of Methodism's founder, John Wesley, Garlinda could help.

And not only could she help, she did so without complaint and with unwavering good humor. On countless occasions I would climb the stairs from the basement of the United Methodist Communications building where the television side of things got done, up to the lofty heights of the news service offices on the floor above and knock on Garlinda's door. Surrounded by an impressive mixture of personal travel photos from around the world and Mickey Mouse memorabilia (Garlinda is a collector extraordinaire of Mickey Mouse "object d'art"), she invariably would motion me in with an enthusiastic wave of her bangle bedecked arm. Quite often she would do so while carrying on an animated telephone conversation and tapping away on her computer. She was a wonder to behold in action.

"What's up?" she would ask as she put the phone down. I would explain the latest broadcast challenge before me and she would be up on her feet in a heartbeat, bustling around her office digging out a document or a phone number or a photo, her brightly colored African print frock rustling around her feet.

Over the years and through the many miles we church-related journalists trek together, Garlinda and I became friends—good friends. Though I was based in New York, when I came to Nashville for a week of television production and could not face one more night in an anonymous hotel, Garlinda offered me refuge in her own home. She would whip up a fabulous bit of traditional southern food and we would eat and chat and laugh long into the night. If I had the good fortune to be around on a weekend, she would invite me along to her church where the congregation welcomed me like a long lost daughter. I suppose in a way I was. It was splendid.

I cannot begin to tell you the gratitude and love I feel for this dear friend who helped me find my way in these early years of life at a national church agency. It was an act of kindness and generosity I know she has shared with countless others as well. But Garlinda gave me something else that has helped keep my faith intact during rough and tumble times when church politics proves heavy going.

"Just remember one thing," she said to me with particular seriousness one afternoon. "Working professionally in the church can be hazardous to your spiritual health. Don't ever confuse your faith and your relationship to God with your professional life and relationship in the institutional church. Keep yourself firmly connected to a local congregation. They will help you remember what matters most."

I have hung on to these words, sometimes for dear life, since that day. Confronting the reality of human frailty in the institutional church is tough, bewildering, and at times demoralizing. More than once I felt sure the sanest response to these perplexing and even poisonous institutional hazards would be to run screaming from the room, never to return. Garlinda's advice has helped me to stick around.

Wherever my specialist communications ministry has taken me—first to New York, then London, and now to Manchester in the north of England—I have tried to keep close ties with a local church congregation. Those faith communities have grounded me, prayed for me, and embodied Christ alive for me during the years I have had the privilege and the challenge of reporting on the global family of God at the best and worst of times.

Garlinda Burton eventually became the head of the United Methodist News Service and then went on to the position she now holds as the top executive for the denomination's Commission on the Status and Role of Women. I feel sad that I see her so infrequently these days. But I smile when I think of her putting her energy, capability, warmth, and courage to work for this area of the church's life. Thank you, Garlinda. Thank you for helping me and so many others keep the faith.

GARY MASON IN NORTHERN IRELAND

It is in the nature of the work of a journalist that you meet people—often in dramatic circumstances—talk with them about profound and intensely personal experiences and beliefs, and then leave—rarely, if ever, to meet them again. I find this very hard. I cannot hear news reports or see a headline about the current hardship in Zimbabwe without worrying about what has happened to the children I interviewed at a mission school there fifteen years ago. They would be grown now, with children of their own. How are they coping? What has happened to all those dreams for the future they shared with me? More than a decade after the war in the Balkans I still think about the Bosnian Muslim woman who stood in the ruins of her front yard and told me how her neighbors had burned her house to the ground and murdered her son. Is Hadijah Petrovitch still living across the fields from those neighbors? Can she let her grandchild play in those fields, confident that landmines planted there during the war no longer threaten her family?

When circumstances do allow me to follow a story over a period of time, it is a gift. Northern Ireland is a half hour plane ride from my home in Manchester. That fact, and the emergence of low-cost airlines, has allowed me to report regularly on events in that troubled part of the world. Methodist minister Gary Mason is one of the people I interviewed during my first trip to Belfast in 1992. Gary stood in the sanctuary of his church beside a pile of charred hymnals, telling me about the realities of ministry in a divided society. Only a few days before, someone had tried to set the church on fire using the hymnals as kindling. It was not the first time it had happened or probably the last.

Gary is a rather unassuming, soft-spoken man. He does not insist on your attention when he walks into the room. First impressions might not lead you to believe that here before you stands a mover and a shaker. You would be wrong.

Throughout the years I have known him I have seen Gary put himself literally on the front line time and time again in the name of reconciliation and peace. Gary's ministry in areas of Belfast where hardline Protestant paramilitaries (self-styled vigilantes) wield enormous power has put Gary right in the midst of people many have written off as irredeemable, worthless men of violence.

The Loyalist Commission, which Gary helped to set up, brings together some of the highest ranking figures in these Protestant paramilitary groups for frank discussions about a peaceful way forward for Northern Ireland. Today this commission has a recognized presence in the peace process.

Gary is the kind of man who put himself directly between feuding Protestant paramilitary factions to resolve a dispute that left a grieving family unable to bury their murdered family member. In October of 2002 Gary Mason walked out of his office at the East Belfast Mission, and straight into the pub where more than a hundred angry Ulster Defense Association paramilitary members were gathered. He announced, "Someday I might be doing your funeral and your family would not want anything to stop it, would they?" Gary left the pub with assurances that the funeral of a man from the rival paramilitary group (the Loyalist Volunteer Force) could take place unimpeded.

These are guys whose idea of keeping the peace in their neighborhood is to shoot unruly teenagers in the knee caps. The fact that Gary is a Methodist minister did not give him any automatic protection or clout. What did make the difference is that he knew them. Gary knew their families. He had put in the time and effort to understand their world and the pressures they faced as fathers, husbands, sons—and providers. He knew exactly what to say and do because he had been alongside them when it was uncomfortable, when things got desperate, and when no one else gave a damn about the people who dished out death.

Gary's commitment to this work certainly has cost him. He confided more than once to me that he was unsure whether he should be bringing his young sons up in Belfast. As a well-educated, talented pastor he could have chosen to serve churches in far kinder conditions. What parent would not worry about raising boys in a culture where social deprivation and violence can combine in such a destructive way?

Gary has stayed. Not to be an apologist or chaplain to the tribe in his sectarian Protestant corner of Belfast, but because he knows, better than most, that real peace for Northern Ireland's Catholics and Protestants will not come solely from official agreements and declarations about putting weapons beyond use. He knows that for real peace to take hold the disenfranchised, marginalized ones must find their way to work, self-worth, and a sense of belonging in a new Northern Ireland no longer organized by sectarian armed conflict. The self-appointed foot soldiers of "The Troubles" will have to see something better and more sustaining in the future to let go of the past. Gary and his ministry team's persistent efforts to build real links in a troubled community one relationship at a time are bringing on the peace that has been so illusive and costly.

Gary lives his calling in a way few of us will ever do, right out on the edge where it is uncomfortable and chaotic and the boundaries are fluid. It is a place where many respectable people are not sure they want their middle-class Methodist minister to be. It is a place of real hopelessness and pain from which few would fault him for walking away. But Gary never has.

Gary taught me that you can love your neighbors while still despising some of their choices and even telling them so. I have witnessed countless incremental victories in Northern Ireland's struggle for peace that have come from Gary Mason's unfailing commitment to this work and the community he has been called to serve. Thank you, Gary, for showing me what it means to stay the course, even when others doubt you, even when you doubt yourself. Thank you for showing me how to hope against hope one day at a time.

SAMSON MUNGURE IN ZIMBABWE

The Rev. Samson Mungure was waiting for me and my film crew at Harare Airport. Flights from New York to Zimbabwe via Brussels, Kenya, Uganda, and Malawi meant we had been traveling for nearly two days straight. I have never felt so physically awful in my life. Samson scooped us up and mercifully deposited us at the Harare Holiday Inn, returning later to explain our itinerary for the next ten days in Zimbabwe.

Fellow producer Hilly Hicks and I were in Africa to film a range of stories including the ground-breaking ceremony of the new Africa University in Old Mutare near the Mozambique border. None of our staff film crews were available for the trip so we were working with a freelance cameraman called Rob and a sound engineer called Tim. Neither had worked with us before nor had any real experience filming a church-related subject.

Samson was our full-time guide. Even though he had oversight responsibility for many pastors and churches in the eastern part of Zimbabwe, he acted as if he had all the time in the world to help us. He patiently transported us across dusty landscapes to remote mission stations and churches. He smoothed the way with officials before we arrived and introduced us to countless people who contributed interviews to our film. It was a good thing he was looking out for us because Hilly and I seemed to spend all our time trying to manage cameraman Rob, who had a propensity for swearing and a vicious nicotine habit that led him sporadically to light up inside church sanctuaries. Hilly and I tried to explain the special sensitivities of church communities to Rob. He just did not seem to get it.

"He's not a United Methodist, is he?" was Samson's only direct comment to me about Rob. "No, he certainly is not," I replied.

Long hours traveling over many days meant we all spent a lot of time together in a small van. As the trip progressed more and more often I noticed Rob scrambling for the front seat next to Samson when we traveled. The two seemed to be having quite in-depth conversations about theology and belief. Those conversations began to spill over into meals as well. Rob was still a handful, but we could not fail to notice that he certainly was engaged by the faith stories we were filming and even more so by his chats with Samson.

Toward the end of our trip, we arrived at a mission station just in time to have lunch with a group of local pastors. All of us, including Tim and Rob, stood in a circle holding hands waiting for the food to be blessed. One of the local pastors turned to Rob and asked him to say the blessing. I shot Hilly a look of bemused surprise, which he immediately returned. Next thing I heard was Rob's hesitant "well, okay" followed by a more confident "let us pray." And he did! You could have knocked me over with a feather.

After the "Amen" I looked over at Samson, who was grinning from ear to ear. Rob crept up behind me a few minutes later and whispered, "Didn't think I had it in me, did ya?"

He was right. I did not think he had it in him. But Samson did. And it made all the difference. When we said our good-byes to Samson, it was Rob who hugged him the hardest and the longest. In those few brief days together Samson reminded me not only to believe in transformation, but invest in it. Rob carried on being a pain in the backside as we continued our filming trip through Zambia and then into what was Zaire, now the Democratic Republic of Congo. But because of Samson, things were just a bit different. We were different together. Samson had shown us all a different way.

These days whenever I hear that someone is going to Zimbabwe on United Methodist Church business, I always ask them to please say "hello" to my friend Samson Mungure. What I really want to ask them to say to him is "thank you."

ANGELA BAKER AND THE CALENDAR GIRLS OF GREAT BRITAIN

Angela Baker opened the door of her picturesque Yorkshire cottage and warmly welcomed me inside. I had come to interview her about the experience of losing her husband to cancer five years before and how, out of the grief and frustration of his death, she and her friends ended up raising over $1.7 million for leukemia research.

"Cup of coffee?" she asked. "Trisha is coming around to say 'hello'." Trisha is Angela's best friend. I am one of hundreds, if not thousands of journalists these two women have spoken to in the years since the news of their nude Women's Institute calendar first hit international headlines. A few minutes later, Trisha breezed in and made us all laugh with a couple of choice stories about what happened in their sleepy little village when Hollywood crews turned up to film their life story for the movie, *Calendar Girls*. Let me just say that Hollywood's idea of traditional Yorkshire landscapes failed to anticipate the pervasive presence of sheep poo.

When the coffees were finished, Trish bowed out to teach a Pilates class and Angela and I sat down for a chat about the faith journey that led her to hell and back when her husband John was diagnosed with non-Hodgkins lymphoma.

"I remember saying to him, 'John, why you?'" she told me. "John said, 'Why not me, Angela'?"

She tells me John Baker was a man devoted to his family, his friends, his work in the Yorkshire Dales National Park, and his Methodist church. He and Angela expected to live out a quiet life in the Yorkshire Dales together enjoying their children and grandchildren. His death at age fifty-four left Angela in bits and pieces she thought would never come back together. Trying to honor John's memory and help her friend laugh again, Trisha suggested they do a Women's Institute calendar to raise money for cancer research. The idea was that together with their WI friends, they would pose in the nude doing traditional crafts such as baking, knitting, and jam-making. They persuaded nine friends to say "yes" and their world has not been the same since.

By the end of the hour-and-a-half interview I had cried and I had laughed and I was completely taken with the vulnerability and gutsyness of Angela and her friends.

I met with Angela and the "Calendar Girls" several times more over the months that followed to chat and film them as they made special appearances raising money for the Leukemia Research Fund. No matter where they went, they made time for every fan who wanted to shake their hands, get an autograph, or tell them about their own loss or battle with cancer. The more time I spent with these women, the more I sensed a goodness about them that was palpable. Everyone I met who was associated with them reflected this same good and generous spirit. Goodness begetting goodness. It was almost weird but it certainly was wonderful. Then it struck me—Deuteronomy 30:19:

> I have set before you life and death, blessings and curses.
> Choose life so that you and your descendants may live.

Angela Baker chose life even in the midst of death. Angela, Trisha, and their friends chose the blessings and banished the curses that can come from the most broken moments of our lives. They refused to let John's life be only about his death. They found the life in his death and then multiplied it a thousandfold. They did not know exactly what they were doing or where it would lead, but they clung on to life and laughter and each other and did something amazing.

Angela's local Methodist pastor has been among those applauding loudest for the Calendar Girls. "God had to be involved," the Rev. Keith Hopper told me. "These women leave a bit of joy behind everywhere they go." I could not agree more.

I was surprised to discover that some in the U.S. church found this story unsuitable for United Methodist church publications. "We can't be seen to be supporting middle-aged women taking their clothes off no matter how worthy the cause," one editor told me when I pitched this story. That was not the only United Methodist rejection I got. Happily not everyone shared this view and in their May/June 2004 issue *Zion's Herald* magazine published my interview with Angela, complete with a photo from the original calendar.

Angela and I are still in touch. She is still choosing life and inspiring others, including me, to hang on to the blessings and shake off the curses that come our way. Thank you, Angela. I am with Rev. Hopper and countless others who are still applauding you—with abandon.

A POSTSCRIPT OF THANKSGIVING

To all the people who have accompanied me on my faith journey, including those who stories I have told above, thank you, God bless and keep you always. I think of you more often than you will ever know.

NINE

FRIENDSHIP EMBODIED AND THE LIFE OF THE SPIRIT

MARTIN E. MARTY

Søren Kierkegaard argued that you cannot learn to swim by being suspended from the ceiling by a belt and in that position reading a book on how to swim. You learn swimming by swimming, by being in the water, perhaps guided by someone with book-learning who can impart wisdom about the venture and about improving technique.

Friendship is like that. Reading a book like this one can enhance the appreciation of friendship and provide counsel about becoming a better friend. Appreciation and counsel are both richer, however, if ideas about the subject are at all points grounded and tested in actual friendship and friendly acts, imparted and received.

Treatises on friendship, one would expect, would crowd the shelves of libraries in the Western world. So widespread, so problematic, so promising is friendship that the lists of deep people who would discuss it should be long. Not so. Of course, the big three "A's" of this part of the world check in with such treatises: Aristotle, Augustine, and Aquinas.

It is Aristotle who teaches readers on so many of his pages that true learning is always connected with practice, conduct, and habit. Augustine translates concerns for friendship into his distinctive Christian patterns. Aquinas, as he set out to synthesize theology and human themes, could hardly have avoided something so vital as friendship, and he took up the task.

So much for the A's. What about the B's, on whom we grew up in Christian theology: Barth, Brunner, Bultmann, Bonhoeffer, Baillie, (von) Balthasar, and so many more? Some of them touched on the subject, Dietrich Bonhoeffer most notably through his letters. Yet we are hard pressed to find full-length works from those B's, to say nothing of the C's through the Z's.

Why is this the case?—which may be a way of asking why a book like this one has its place. In my observation, as philosophers or theologians pick their subject matters, they choose uncompromised and grand subjects. Think of the polarity of "hate" and "love." They are grand, billboard-sized themes that most candidates for Great Books have to take up. Similarly, "life" and "death" or "war" and "peace" are subjects that merit and receive major treatment. In such combinations and contrasts, friendship comes through as a pastel, half-committed part of life, too big to be dismissed but not titanic enough to evoke profound thoughts.

Happily—an adverb we find ourselves necessarily using too rarely in this unhappy new century—friendship is finally drawing more attention, this book also being an instance illustrating that. Not that the last word has been said on love/hate, peace/war, life/death; changing contexts elicit new research and writing. However, publics are learning to cherish themes that lie between the grand extremes. And as thinkers explore them, they find unforeseeably rich promptings.

Take music, for example. Historically, after Plato, philosophers and, before Karl Barth, theologians tended to think of it as an adornment of life, part of its sonic décor, but not the real stuff of existence. Then one tunes in to Johann Sebastian Bach, who knew what he was talking about when he described music as God's greatest gift to God's sorrowing creatures, to give them a joy worthy of their destiny. Cannot one say the same about friendship on a par with music?

Take politics, for a second example. Here more philosophers and periodically many theologians have addressed its meanings. Still it is a stepchild among the natural subjects of concern. Why? Politics does not save souls, does not make sad hearts glad, or provide final answers. Politics may be God-blessed, but it is a human invention by people who know that the alternatives to politics are chaos and the jungle. Politics, like friendship, involves trading, settling for partial victories and not always total defeats, demanding compromise, and helping minimize the violence that is native to human history. Cannot one say the same about friendship on a par with politics?

I got into the friendship writing business rather accidentally, contingency being one of the main prompters in my vocation. After my first wife died, I was given to reflect on the experience that took her from us and all but overwhelmed me and mine a quarter century ago. I was later called to write about our family experiences, and chose not to give a clinical accounting of the toll of cancer or a revealing portrait of that wonderful, private woman. Beyond the predictable and always abundant measures of grace, hope, and comfort that come with the retching after chemo and the long night watches that imply "good-bye, soon!" she and I agreed that we were most favored by friendship, which is not an abstraction: call it friends.

AVAILABILITY

Friends had and have a most marked characteristic that I associated with a favored word, *disponibillité*, which I learned from French philosopher Gabriel Marcel. All his translators and interpreters agree that the word is finally untranslatable. Still, one can catch nuances in it of "being at the disposal of," best seen as "being available to." *Disponibilité* can mean what I call "creative schedule interruption," the symbolic open door at a professor's office, the turn and showing of her face to a patient by a doctor, a coach singling out for special notice the runty and inept but determined soccer player. It can also mean not just a physical posture with psychological meanings, but can be a philosophy itself.

Friends, truly friends, knew when to call on my wife and family and me and when not to call; when to leave with her as a gift and token a rose or perfume or scarf or other signals of feminine life when chemo was taking its visual and physical toll. Friends, real friends, knew when to offer a ride or some house-sitting or something so constant that I wrote a column about it and let it symbolize friendship: dropping off a casserole before dinner or, reading the situation right some nights, staying to eat with us. Friends, most notably three pastoral "L's," who did not write books on friendship like the "A's" did, Lueking, Landahl, and Lundin, were uncanny in their ability to be available with properly timed intercession and comfort.

After a column or two that I wrote out of these experiences of being befriended I was asked by a publisher to write a short book, and I did: Friendship was the unimaginative-sounding title that was exactly to the point. Being a professor meant that I was ready to read the greats on friendship while figuratively being suspended in mid-air, and that readiness is what led me to the futile search for good old books on friendship.

WHERE AGAPE AND EROS MEET

If "friendship" looked bland between the gross subjects like "love" and "hate," it carried a bit of burden for a person with my training. Colleagues of my vintage cut their theological teeth on writings from a notable revival of Luther in Sweden. This was not the scholastic dulled-down Luther of the seventeenth-century traducers, but raw, radical Luther. Among the most influential interpretations was Bishop Anders Nygren's *Agape and Eros*. It was a stylized, Procrustean-embedding work of great vigor and clarity and overstatement.

To this day I am grateful for Nygren's way of showing how God's agape is our great befriending. The love that this Greek word connotes is "spontaneous, unmotivated, undeserving, gracious" action. God comes to us thus in Jesus Christ, we learned and I still learn. And humans can be, they get to be, compromised by still valid transmitters of such love that does not seek an object but works indiscriminately on stranger and belonger, deserving and undeserving. So far so good.

Nygren was at such pains to be sure that agape would not be compromised and that radical Luther's reading of the apostle Paul stand in brash and bold relief, that he taught us his readers to be nervous about eros. We tracked through ages of Christian history theologians who tied down God by connecting divine mercy with human striving, the human enchainment of God. Such eros love can compromise or devastate the concept of divine grace. It is at this point, however, that the Swedish bishop overstepped the bounds and neglected the evidence. Biblical thought recognized and encouraged human desire. "If with all your hearts you truly seek me, you shall also surely find me." That seeking is erotic, but the effort does not tie God down.

Similarly, eros has its place in human affairs, not only in erotic (as usually defined) and marital love, but also in plain, old, quotidian, everyday friendship. Without it there would not, will not, be friendship. A friend seeks, strives, needs, transacts. If agape is unmotivated, friendship at its best and worst sees something of value in the object called the Other.

We speak of "falling in love," a precipitous act that cannot be accounted for—just try to do more than tell stories about it—and cannot easily be climbed up from or out of. Fortunately, lovers often acquire sanity and direction again as time "heals" erotic love.

We do not speak of "falling into friendship." Most humans more likely climb into it. Of course, there are surprises: "What does she see in that group of friends, and what do they see in her?" Or: "We were among the few marooned at our college over Thanksgiving break so six of us got together and played games, sang songs, drank beer [we were twenty-one!] and now we are forty-two and our gang is still in touch by e-mail, at reunions, or whenever anyone needs us."

Friendships that endure also are based in generosity. Here as so often one must qualify an affirmation: some people remain friends to the Other because the Other has needs or, worse, "is needy." She makes constant demands and is incapable of starting with concern for the other. The more you feed the appetite that seeks someone on whom to be dependent, the more dependent he grows. The more you elicit, encourage, or merely tolerate criticism, the more emboldened the other will be to criticize. Still, amid it all, friendship endures.

SOMETHING THEOLOGICAL, SOMETHING SPIRITUAL

Say something theological or spiritual. I hear that whispered by the editors over my shoulder. You are being practical, mundane: where is the Spirit in all this, they would ask.

Answer: everywhere. God, who sinks God's hearing in the deafness of mortals, is visible invisibly in the call of the neighbor, presents God's self in the ordinary. Jesus' word about it is "what you have done to the least of my brothers [and sisters], you have done to me." Refusing the bid by the lonely for friendship is repudiating the call of Christ. Failing to add to the world's reservoir of resources for friendship is an assault on divine creation, a wonder achieved by a God who seeks company, and has said so.

Friends have many uses, a word that one brings up with a tinge of nervousness. Cannot friendship be like agape, with friends never counting the cost or reckoning how one will be better off for cultivation? I have often observed that it is hard to sustain, not among the famous but to and from the celebrity. A person of fame may have friends. Most celebrities—not all, as I will illustrate—tend to have fawning claques.

They have to be uncritical, at least to the celebrity's face. They fear a loss of status and a move into exile if they engage in any criticism. They surround the celebrity, guard access to her, push others away, brag about their place, and engage in praise.

Friends would not be friends if their relation to the Other were not based on some measure of liking and likeability. However, precisely, a friend may say to someone like me (picture me having enough fame to qualify for this befriended role), "Marty, this time you went too far. Back off." "Get off your high horse; who do you think you are?" "Have you thought about how that action looks or, more, what that action is and does?" "Straighten up and fly right."

Because these things get said, even though they form a test to the ego and the friendship, the ones who have said it have credentials to be available in another way. The celebrity is never sure whether what sounds like the language of friendship is that, or is flattery designed to better the position of the flatterer. The friend comes with measures of authenticity that mean more when words like these are heard: "You look down today. What's up?" Or: "Can I lift the heavy end of whatever that weight is that appears to be on your mind?" Or: "Shall we take a walk and converse?" Or: "Yes, you can call me at three in the morning. I was in my REM [rapid eye movement] stage and am a bit woozy, but as soon as my head clears, I'll be right over."

The silliest and most unspiritual thing one hears about a friendship is that it is a "perfect friendship." Such can exist only if one suppresses all feelings for the Other, wants to be blinded or delusional, or has bad taste. Theologically and spiritually, we are talking about friends as part of a broken universe. I have liked Luther's saying that "God rides the lame horse; God carves the rotten wood." So God makes something enhancing—back to Bach: to give us a joy worthy of our destiny—by offering us friends.

Clarinetist Artie Shaw at age ninety was asked why he quit playing clarinet at age fifty, though he then was as near perfection as a clarinetist could get. "That's it," he replied. "They told me I was as near perfection as I could get, so why burn out, trying for more?" "How are you now?" Shaw, nursing a replacement knee, said: "Well, I'm not perfect, but even when I was perfect I wasn't perfect." There is a whole philosophy of history (and of friendship) tucked into that phrase.

FRIENDSHIP DIVINE

Some years ago I was a resource at a conference of Christian young people, assigned the task of speaking on divine friendship. I found a book, a really rare example, on this kind of theme, as I mentioned earlier, by a German theologian named Schnackenburg. I forget the details of his little treatise, but I found that the theologian successfully portrayed God as friend, God in Jesus as friend. So much did he, or I derivatively, stress that God's presence refracted through the image of Jesus onto the other, meant that instead of singing the hymn literally, "What a friend we have in Jesus," we could sing, nonblasphemously, "What a Jesus we have in a friend."

Jesus formed a company. Company = *cum* (with) + *panis* (bread), the people with whom you share bread and form a table. It is hard to sustain friendship without the employment of a table, food and drink, and conversation. More radically, Jesus described a friend as someone who would give his or her life for another. Friends have done that for centuries, and will keep doing it. Jesus described effective life as being based in forgiveness. Friendship is an exacting relationship that demands forgiving and offers countless opportunities for providing it.

ASSIGNMENT: NAME SOME EXEMPLARY FRIENDS

Being an obedient Swiss-American given to scrupulous following of assignments, let me say that I noticed two substantive elements expected of our essays. One, they should stress the spiritual and the theological. Two, they should include recountings of actual friendships, in which the spiritual shines. So, finally, off to "two" we go.

Here's a sample of a friendship between true unequals, especially in status. Louis J. Sieck was president of Concordia Seminary in St. Louis, which I was attending in its better days before some unfriendly sorts dis-welcomed our kind. Sieck had been pastor of a large congregation in the city. Rumor among seminarians had it that he sported a diamond stick-pin in his ascot worn almost daily behind his white-piped vest, inside cutaway coat, above striped morning-trousers, because he had profited from a semispiritual venture. When the Catholic archbishop tired of holding last rites for all the local mafia sorts, it was said that he called on his friend Sieck to inter some of them with Lutheran blessings. If that tale is not true, do not tell me; I do not want to be deprived of such a tale by the truth.

Sieck was not an intellectual, but he was a pastor: gruff though he could be, his was a soft heart. I edited the student magazine and checked in monthly with him to discuss its contents. He never censored us, though he might well have. It happened that in my final year when I was scheduled, they told me, to be a pastor for a term to Baltic-area displaced persons in London, half the faculty noticed that we had used the school paper, library, bookstore, and more, to invent and propagate the lore of a fake theologian, Franz Bibfeldt. Some seminarians used comment on him to elicit reply remarks about his influence from some of the slower faculty who bluffed their way into acquaintance with the writings of this nonexistent person.

At ten at night, in his home, where I needed a friend, Sieck asked me: "Is that a satire on one of us or on all of us?" Honestly, it was a satire on "the system." "That's how I read it," he said.

Now, it happens that he and I had developed a friendship. We had found mutual pastoral and theological interests. He had smuggled back to a little circle of us amateur theologians some first printings of some early postwar publications that were down our line. But as for that night, he still had the problem of some faculty pressures with which to deal. Needless to say, as they caught on, they felt they needed revenge. The first half of the faculty did not see itself parodied, and enjoyed our publications. But this half decided that I was "too immature and irresponsible" to represent us Lutherans in the UK. (They had that one right!) Some wanted me expelled. Others simply decreed that I should ripen under the tutelage of a mature and responsible senior pastor, to whom I would be curate-style assistant. Fine. Sieck and Company sent me to a pastor whose parish had written into its call that a person in my post must work on a doctorate. I went, and because of that assignment, reluctant though I was, I headed toward the doctorate. Oh, and I was not to publish more on Dr. Bibfeldt. As I left, he put his hand on my shoulder and uttered the only profanity I ever heard from him: "I just want you to know, young man, that this Bibfeldt incident is the funniest damn thing I've seen since I've been president."

Forget now friendships among equals, that have no hierarchical or status boundaries to cross. It sounds old-fashioned to speak of a "best friend," and it may even sound discriminatory against other good friends. However, my seminary room mate Dean Lueking and I would add up the number and quality of encounters—almost weekly for most years in the last sixty years—and find that we had prosecuted a friendship that the Martys consider immeasurably rewarding. We have had moments of confiding and confessing that we will carry to our graves, but would not trade them for much of anything on this side of the grave. Recommendations: in whatever tradition you find yourself, look up a book of confession and use one as a liturgy between yourself and a friend. Our families celebrate the table at Thanksgiving, Christmas, and Easter. We have vacationed together. Note: vacations can be real tests of friendship!

When the church body to which we belonged was breaking apart or breaking us off, friend Lueking was at the crosshairs of the gun-sights of the party whose ways we could not square with Christian mandates, norms, or promises. Their leadership was even finding cause to cost the church body and his parish on their opposing sides hundreds of thousands of dollars that could have gone to good causes. How did he sustain himself through the siege? God helped. So, I think, did human friendship. The Luekings and the Martys relaxed by monthly hearings of the Chicago Symphony, always preceded by a dinner in a club atop the symphony hall. The two spouses and I would chat while Dean was parking. We would conspire to enforce a three-minute rule when he returned.

He would arrive and say, "You'll never believe what they did to our congregation today . . ." We would believe, because that's what they regularly did. He had three minutes to tell the story, at the end of which the wine would arrive and the food followed. He certifies that this kind of discipline imposed by friends was liberating, a reminder that there is more to life than ecclesiastical warfare. Lueking also had an uncanny ability to know when and how to arrive for pastoral counsel to the clinics at the time of the dreaded verdicts after X-rays and CAT scans, always imparting realistic hope along with the bread and the cup: com+pany.

LATER-IN-LIFE FRIENDSHIPS

This has been until now a narrowly Lutheran, and therefore sectarian-sounding, little essay. I think our prescriptions included the call to reach beyond the provincial in an interfaith world. So I'll reach across the boundaries to point to two enduring friendships that belong to the serendipitous, contingent, accidental range of circumstances. In the height of the first far right and fundamentalist assaults on the body politic, Hollywood producer Norman Lear, of whom I had heard but whose programs, capped by *All in the Family*, I had not seen, phoned. He was forming People for the American Way and was told that my studies and interests might lead me to a zone of mutual concern.

Lear looked me up during the last half year of my wife's life. I was pledged not to leave Chicago a single day in 1981, wanting to be available to my terminally ill wife. So he on some occasions flew in, and we got together for an hour near our home. I did not join the board of PFAW, since as a sometime journalist I do not join or sign on with any causes, needing to be free to criticize. But we grew close.

The winter after my wife died, Lear invited me to take part in planning a PBS special on George Washington's 250th birthday. I knew nothing about what I was doing, but I trusted my new friend. In the bleak winter after her death, my dean having suggested that I not teach for a quarter and other friends having urged me to write, I took time away from class and did write *A Cry of Absence*. At five in the morning I would turn on the heat and look out the window as snow fell—and start writing.

One does not live by mourning and the sight of winter landscapes alone. In those months I was surprised to be called by Lear to be a sometimes house guest in California, and to "work on" some scripts, something which I actually did. I would fly in on Sunday night, have long, long breakfasts with Lear and others who were guests, and then go through the motions of amateur script-writing. The California sun worked its own spell. Only later did it occur to me that some if not most of this inviting was the mark of a generous friend who was offering me alternatives in a low season. That friendship has endured, and later with my second wife at table we and Lear and other new friends started discussions that have to be called theological.

Spouse Harriet remembers how at the first of these occasions, before the wine list arrived, Lear leaned forward and said, "All right, Marty, tonight I want you to tell me about your God. Take all the time you need, but tell me." This from a man tabbed as "Mr. Secular Humanist" by mis-portrayers. I did "tell," but only if and as he told, and we keep telling, in a larger circle of friends that he summons and entertains. This circle is one of several that "grew" in the most recent one-third of our lives.

Telling of that might sound as if we were dealing with celebrity, but by my definition he was famous, not a celebrity, because he is anticlaque (as is another in that circle, Bill Moyers, with whom theological dimensions of friendship are always prime). Both welcome criticism, and expect their friends to, too. I would like to think that these paragraphs are not name-dropping or out-of-school; both of them have "gone public" with their interpretations of this friendship.

Some of Harriet's and my friends have been such for more than a half century. They and we are available to each other, and tell each other secrets and eat and cry and conspire and laugh together. Harriet and I have not moved beyond any of these. Yet we welcome just as much the new company, some of them Muslim, more of them Jewish: novelists, judges, musical comedy writers, and more. One thing I have learned from them: all open and engaged friendships have a spiritual dimension nurtured on questions that cannot be suppressed. Why would we want to, every one of these friends would ask. They and we will keep seeking answers. Were we ever to become sure of the answers, our friendships would be sorely tested, because we would not need each other any more. We could live on divine agape, but human eros is also a gift. Like music. Like politics. Like everything that matters, even when not scaled to the gigantic reach of themes like "love" and "hate."

TEN

FREEDOM FOUND THROUGH FRIENDSHIP

STEPHEN K. MCCENEY

Ever since I can remember, friends have been important to me. They are like the *prana* that yogis refer to in India, part of the "life force" that runs through our bodies. Once I make a friend, it seems to be for life. My fourth grade teacher called me about nineteen years ago to say she was passing through Denver and wanted to give me some of my "most memorable compositions" that I had written and that for some reason she had saved. I was thirty years old at the time. I was surprised but we had a pleasant, albeit brief, reunion at the train station. She excitedly handed me a stack of these childhood masterpieces. One of them was entitled "My Friends." The following is an unedited version.

> January 1968
>
> I have a lot of friends that I like. My best friend is Mark Roosevelt whose personality I enjoy very much. He's very funny and is always making jokes, which in my opinion are remarkably funny.
>
> Another one of my very best friends is Steve Canton. You should know him pretty well. He also is quite funny and very energetic. I also like Danny Walsh who is in our little group. Mark Murphy and Jimmy McCarthy are also in it. Mark and Jimmy are very entertaining also. We all have fun when we're together.

These are the guys whose homes were like my home and mothers were like my mother. We played little league together, went to proms together, and spent hours in detention together. Then came the weddings and children and so on. Even though we now live in different cities, I have had dinner with all of these guys, often as a group, many times in the last few years and they are still "very entertaining."

HEALTH CHALLENGES DEEPEN BONDS OF FRIENDSHIP

More importantly, we were all together just last month for Jimmy McCarthy's wife's funeral. Her name was Sarah. It was a sad occasion, of course, as she was only forty-seven years old and has left two fantastic young sons and a wonderful partner behind. I had the good fortune of being with her the week before she died and was able to spoil her and the family a little for a day, preparing food and just being there. What a wonderful gift. Her funeral was like a huge reunion for many of us, as the bonds of friendship in the Irish Catholic community I grew up in are very strong and important, not only for sharing the joys but of course to help us through the losses.

While Jim and I have been friends since kindergarten, Sarah and I had become fast friends since they were married almost nineteen years ago. We had a special affinity for each other. Our bond was to grow stronger as life's challenges began to present themselves. In 1985, my life partner, John, and I were diagnosed with HIV. In the beginning we were scared to share this with our friends and family. Gradually we let people into our circle for much needed support. We lived in Denver and the McCarthys lived in Washington, D.C., but we would get together over the holidays and during vacations.

Around this time Sarah shared with us that she was working on experimental AIDS treatments in the research lab at the National Institutes of Health (NIH). Knowing this, we finally shared our news with Sarah and Jim. Sarah kept encouraging us to get involved with the treatment protocols in Washington, but at the time it seemed overwhelming for us to think about treatment in another city. A couple of years before John died, Jim called to tell me that Sarah had been diagnosed with breast cancer. Of course, we were saddened by the news, but at the time John was very sick and we had all we could handle. Yet these significant health challenges that we now shared seemed to strengthen our bond, and over the years it grew much stronger.

Sarah ended up overcoming two occurrences of cancer early on, and then moved into remission for six years. A few years after John died, I went home to Washington for Thanksgiving and visited with Sarah. She shared with me the news that her cancer had metastasized to her spine and lymph system. The prognosis was not good, but Sarah was very matter of fact and had decided to undergo the most aggressive treatment they offered; a bone marrow transplant from her twin sister. It was a grueling experience she endured for almost a year. Thankfully, she was to regain her health and establish a respectable quality of life for another five years. Sarah McCoy McCarthy was an inspiration to me, and I dedicate this essay in her memory.

GOD'S PRESENCE IN FAMILY AND FRIENDS

As John's illness began to manifest, and he became sicker, I became more frightened. I was scared of what was going to happen in this process. Could I handle taking care of him and taking care of my other responsibilities at the same time? Could I make the appropriate medical decisions when the time came? Would I be able to administer his IV medications? Could I cope with his fears? Could I deal with his family's fears? How was I going to live without him? He was my closest friend and companion with whom I wanted to spend the rest of my life. I loved him deeply and we were very happy. Was I going to be able to care for him and take care of my own health at the same time? Would our friends and family be there for us? And my biggest fear: I was going to be alone and die alone, after all this.

And now it was really being tested. I asked myself, "Where is God in all of this?" I searched for and found God in my prayers and meditation. I became increasingly enveloped in a sense of trust that God would be there for us as we went through this painful trial. But even that is not much to hold onto when faced with such brutal and real circumstances.

I gradually became convinced of God's presence, not only in the deafening and massive silence between moments, but manifested physically every day in the form of family members, old friends, new friends, and even strangers. I began to see that every time we needed something, whether it was medical assistance, a hot meal, emotional support, or financial assistance, it was always there. Sometimes it came from loved ones I would have expected to be there. My mom and my sisters all made trips to come and help us. Old friends stopped over and kept in constant touch. My brother and his girlfriend were always there. It was the comfort and relief of loved ones. But sometimes it came from places we never would have expected, from people we hardly knew, acquaintances from church or support groups, near strangers connected by the universal human quality of compassion.

FEAR, TRUST, AND FRIENDSHIP

Nevertheless, through that entire period I continued to be frightened. Of course there were times when the fear was less intense than others, but it was ever present throughout, right up to John's death.

Oddly enough, the real tests have come since he died, and the true revelations of friendship as well. During his illness I really did not have time to acknowledge the insights I described above, it was just a matter of getting through each day. When it was all over I woke up one day and thought to myself, what the heck just happened? Losing people we love is very surreal; it feels like a bad dream. For the first three years I was in a fog, trying to find my way in the world again. Once again it was my friends who rallied around me and gave meaning and love to my life. But this never seemed enough. Were my friends going to be there like a partner would if I got ill and died?

For the next three years I frantically put energy into finding a mate to fill the emptiness and to grant me the security I had felt with John. The loneliness was palpable. I wanted someone who would be there for me if something happened. I can see now I was still being driven by fear and lack of trust in the divine order of things. In retrospect, I believe I naively expended a lot of physical and emotional energy only to learn more of love's lessons the hard way. The universe works on its own timetable unbeknownst to us.

Then in the spring of 2000, illness struck home again. My worst fears seemed to be coming true. I developed a significant gastrointestinal problem, probably due to the medications in combination with the HIV. My symptoms included severe stomach pain and discomfort and an almost complete inability to digest food and absorb the appropriate nutritional value from it. Soon I had lost more than thirty-five pounds, and I felt and looked like a seriously ill person. There was a lot of uncertainty surrounding my diagnosis, but I was fearful something bad was happening. It was an unavoidable and dreaded feeling reflected in my family and friends as well. I could see the worry in their eyes when they looked at me.

I was unable to work for about a year. Recovery continued slowly for years as I gradually allowed myself increased responsibilities. During this period, I spent a great deal of time alone. I was either immobile on the couch because of the pain I experienced after eating, in meditation, or walking at least three times a day because, despite the pain, the exercise facilitated digestion. At this point, with all the walking I was doing I was inspired to get a dog. A friend and I went to an animal shelter where I found my current best friend, Annie, a beautiful and extremely affectionate Australian cattle dog. She has provided years of comfort and companionship and, I am convinced, physical and spiritual healing. Her previous owners abused her so we were both in need of unconditional love at the time. So here I was as I had feared, sick and alone—well, almost.

I have always thought of myself as someone with lots of enduring and strong friendships, but I really never knew how much they meant to me until John's illness. Deep down inside, I didn't really trust that these friends truly loved me and would be there if I really needed them. After all, isn't that a lot to ask? Aren't people busy enough worrying about navigating their own lives without having to carve out a special and specific spot for worrying about me?

What I have learned through all of these challenges is that my friends are always there for me—during John's illness, after his death, through my frenetically seeking a replacement partner, and now when I was really in trouble.

I was very ill. I could hardly take care of myself but I did manage, with the help and love of my family and friends. Once again they showed up with food, rides to the doctor, emotional support, and companionship. Again the friends surrounding me were old and new alike. One friend in particular, Leslie, comes to mind. Leslie was a friend from yoga. (I have been practicing yoga with a local community for more than fourteen years. This discipline has provided tremendous tools for coping and staying as healthy as possible, and has given me another incredible support system.) We had not known each other for very long but had shared some very personal conversations when I became ill. Her loving presence was dedicated, consistent, unexpected, and lasting. I think it was through that bout of illness that I finally began to trust that my friendships were sincere, honest, and real. It occurred to me through my friends' influence and inspiration that God was just as real. Through their love and kindness God was with me every day.

THE ENERGY OF LOVE IN FRIENDSHIP

Another aspect of friendship is that it is reciprocal and exponential. Each act of compassion we choose to make towards another creates benefit and love for both parties, for the giver and for the receiver. Furthermore, the love that is created is multiplied by the synergistic effect of these two souls coming together. It brings to mind the biblical saying, "whenever two or more of you are gathered in [Jesus'] name there is love." I know what amazing gifts my friends have given me but I also know that I have given them equal blessings.

This principle was vividly brought home to me with a powerful experience I had with another dear friend, Father Marty. Marty was a Catholic priest who was instrumental in my making peace with the Catholic Church and who had a tremendous influence over my spiritual growth. He was dying of AIDS and I often visited him. The night before he died we were together and I held his hand in the silence feeling sad but at peace. By this time Marty was ready to die. He looked over at me and in tears told me I was an angel sent to him by God. Ironically, I was just thinking the same thing about him, and as I looked into his eyes all I could see was the light of God. He died on Christmas Day, four months after John did.

A few years into my recovery from my gastrointestinal problem, I received distressing news about my immune system. Apparently, my T-cells, a critical measure of immune functioning, had dropped significantly. This meant that I was extremely immunocompromised and that, although my medication regimen was keeping the virus at bay, it was now unable to keep my immune system at a safe level or to restore my immune functioning. When I shared this news with Sarah, she immediately made arrangements to have me seen at the NIH AIDS clinic to be evaluated for an experimental immune boosting treatment. This time I accepted and I have been working with NIH for the last three years. No one is sure what the outcome will be, but for now the treatment has raised my immune functioning to a safer level and I am stable.

Aside from the medical benefits, the true gift of being in the protocol has been traveling to Washington on a regular basis and spending lots of quality time with my friends and family there. I grew up in Washington as the fourth child in a family of six children, and we had about twenty-eight first cousins. We lost our father when we were quite young, which brought us close together from that point on. I still have all my siblings and their spouses plus twelve beautiful nieces and nephews. My mom lives in the house we grew up in, so I am able to stay with her the six to twelve times per year I go back to the clinic at the NIH. Many of my relatives and extended family, as well as friends, still live in the area, so I am surrounded by love and support whether I am undergoing a treatment, which is much like chemotherapy, or I am just returning for a checkup and lab work. My family, including my mom, is very lucky in that we not only love each other because of our blood kinship, but we really enjoy being with each other. I feel very close to and supported by my family, as I do my old childhood friends.

Another huge bonus about my frequent trips to the NIH was that Sarah and I, and sometimes Jim, would see each other often. She and I would regularly have meals together at the hospital cafeteria, always comparing notes on each other's health status. Sarah learned that her cancer had reoccurred about a year and a half previous. We would complain about our treatments, their side effects, our frustration with the health care system, and how much our diseases interfered with our lives. We shared our fears, hers of never seeing her boys grow up to be men, mine of never finding a partner again. But most of all we were comrades on a similar journey who could admire and support each other's courage. I miss her terribly.

Throughout this trial, my spiritual practice has evolved into something deeper and more sincere. I am forever moved by my friends' loyalty and inspired by the depth of their caring. Our relationships are spirit in action, the manifestation of God in all of us. The energy of love in friendship is the presence of the divine. With each kind action, my friends have shown me God's love, and this has cemented my faith in the divine. I am no longer afraid to die alone. I no longer believe in alone. I am no longer frightened. I have been blessed.

So now it is almost five months after Sarah died and I will return to Washington and the NIH in three weeks for a checkup and blood work. After my clinic visit, I will go to a fiftieth birthday party celebration for her husband Jimmy, Steve Canton, and Danny Walsh. The festivities will take place at the home of the Mark Murphys. These are all the guys mentioned in my fourth grade composition that my teacher felt so compelled to bring to me—my friends.

ELEVEN

A Dialogue between Two Friends

M. KENT MILLARD and DONALD E. MESSER

The intriguing mystery of friendship prompts one to wonder why some human relationships develop and endure over decades while others either simply do not happen or fade over short periods of time. In the currency of life one encounters many interesting people, but only a few connections take on special permanency and depth that result in lifelong friendships.

THE MYSTERY OF FRIENDSHIP

MESSER: Illustrative of the latter has been our friendship. Kent, as I recall, we were both seventeen-year-olds when we "accidentally" met at Boy's State in South Dakota. Twice a day we lined up outside our dormitory for a flag saluting ceremony, and by alphabetical chance Messer and Millard were forced to stand side by side. I do not remember who stood on my left side, but I first got acquainted with you because you repeatedly failed to respond to roll calls. American Legion officials would shout out "Marshall Millard" and I would have to poke you because you were accustomed only to using your middle name of "Kent." Such a strange beginning to a lifelong friendship—a patriotic semi-military event—truly an unlikely place for two future civil rights activists, social justice theologians, and prophetic pastors to meet.

Spinning off from that unexpected encounter have been nearly fifty years of the richest relationship any person could ever enjoy. We became college classmates, debate partners, campus politicians, best men at each other's weddings, seminary colleagues, and ordained ministers. Once you even lost a college scholarship, because you stood up for me when the university was seeking to dismiss me because of a controversial campus newspaper article I wrote!

You and your wife, Minnietta, befriended me throughout my first year of seminary when I was fifteen hundred miles away from my fiancé, Bonnie. Later we marched together in Selma, protested the war in Vietnam, campaigned in the church for the rights of gays and lesbians, and worked for an AIDS-free world. Our families became the best of friends, as we celebrated the birth of our children (our son is named Kent Donald!), the accomplishments of our wives and each other, and the growth of our offspring into mature adulthood.

As brothers, bonded not by blood but by love, we challenged one another, cried with one another, and cherished life's miracles together. You have always been beside me, whether we were campaigning for the ratification of the Panama Canal treaties, or more recently when we journeyed to India to help combat HIV and AIDS.

I hesitate to call our relationship a "holy friendship," since I fear confusing the secular and the sacred, and because, frankly, it seems a bit presumptuous, if not irreligious. On the other hand, I count our friendship a mysterious and precious gift that God has given me. How did this happen?

MILLARD: Don, I think that we became friends by the grace of God but we grew as lifelong friends because of our common commitments and values.

I once read that people do not become close to one another by looking at each other but by looking together in the same direction. When people focus their attention, action, and commitments in the same direction, they are drawn together through their joint activities to reach common goals.

We have looked together in the same direction of renewing the church for the sake of the transformation of the world for the past fifty years and in the process have been drawn into a deep and lasting friendship.

When we were in seminary together in the 1960s we focused on supporting Dr. Martin Luther King's civil rights leadership and found ourselves marching together in the voter rights demonstrations in

Selma, Alabama. In March, 1965, Rev. James Reeb, a Unitarian minister from Boston was killed on the streets of Selma following a voting rights march and many of the civil rights marchers from the north returned to the safety of their homes. King called Harold DeWolf, his major professor at Boston University and asked if he could enroll any seminary students to come and march with the residents of Selma for voting rights. I will always remember being in DeWolf's class with you when he invited us to go to Selma and support King's work.

I know that I would not have had the courage to go on that march if it had not been for your friendship and encouragement. I realized that a pastor from Boston had just been killed for doing what we were going to do, but knowing that I was going with my best friend and not going alone gave me the courage to march in the Selma demonstration.

Before the march we were told that we should march arm in arm with another person so that if they pulled one person out of the line to beat, they would have to pull two persons out of the line and no one would be beaten alone. They told us to pair up, and an African American woman came over to me and said "Sonny, you look scared." I said "Ma'am, I am scared!" She responded, "You march with me and you will be alright." I did march with her each day we were there and no one was pulled out of the line and beaten.

Don, we focused together on the goal of helping to achieve voting rights for African Americans and found ourselves drawn together by our common commitment. I have heard that men who have been in foxholes together during war become lifelong friends because of their common commitment to each other and to the cause for which they are willing to give their lives. In some ways, we became lifelong friends because of our common commitments for which we were also willing to give our lives.

THE MEANING OF FRIENDSHIP

MESSER: Some persons, of course, are famous for the multiple friendships they collect. Most politicians, thanks to a unique mixture of personality, power, and philosophy, typically develop deep loyalties that sustain and strengthen them both in victory and defeat. Illustrative is the charisma of former President Bill Clinton that enabled him to collect a wide range of persons who became known as the "Friends of Bill." With a gift of making each person feel very special, Clinton was able to transform these ties into a potent political force.

Of course, friendships based primarily on politics or power can quickly fade. Some persons pretend friendships in order to leverage influence or gain advantages, but in reality these relationships lack lasting bonds of caring that can survive a career downturn or personal crisis. Much truth resides in the old adage of Walter Winchell, "A real friend walks in when the rest of the world walk out." Or as Judith Viorst says, close friends are persons who "come if we call them at two in the morning."[1]

MILLARD: Don, I remember when my wife, Minnietta, had major surgery about twenty-five years ago. I prayed with her before she went into surgery and then went to the hospital waiting room to wait for the doctor's report of how her surgery came out. I remember sitting in that room all alone, and fearful thoughts crept into my mind. "What if they discovered cancer? What if her heart acted up and she died? What if the surgeon made a devastating mistake?"

I was sitting there trying to put these thoughts out of my mind when you walked in. You had cancelled important meetings at Dakota Wesleyan University where you were president so you could come and sit with me during Minnietta's surgery. You will never know how much that meant to me. When you walked into that waiting room my anxiety level decreased. We talked about Minnietta and her surgery and your presence helped me let go of my fears.

I don't remember anything that you said but simply the fact that you were there to wait with me made all the difference in the world. You walked in the room and my fears walked out. I thank God that Minnietta's surgery was totally successful, but I also thank God for a friend who came to comfort an anxious husband simply by his loving presence.

Several years later your wife, Bonnie, had major surgery and Minnietta and I flew to Denver to wait with you and your family for the successful outcome of her surgery. It occurred to me that friends are simply those who make a commitment to be with each other in good times and in challenging times.

Recently, when your wonderful mother passed away, you invited me to conduct her funeral service. I remembered how she often called me her "other son" because we were together so often we seemed like brothers.

I thank God that we do not have to travel through our life's journey alone; God gives us friends, spouses, partners, and colleagues to walk the journey with us. As I think about my life journey, I know that it has been enriched by your friendship, especially during the difficult times of my life.

THE MIRAGE OF FRIENDSHIP

MESSER: Personally, I have been blessed with wonderful long-term friendships, but I also have experienced the heart-breaking pain of discovering that some relationships I thought qualified as "true friendships" were really mirages that quickly evaporated in the desert moments of my life and career. Like sand in my soul, I have grieved the "loss of friends" that in reality were interested only in gaining and manipulating my trust.

For nearly thirty years I served as a university or graduate theological seminary president. Tragically academia in particular attracts some people who care for others only when it is to their advantage. Intense conflicts and tensions are endemic to the structures and systems. Cynics joke that faculties fight so bitterly because what they fight about is so insignificant, but, regardless, the struggle is real and the injuries inflicted by word and deed are painful.

Early on in my career as a university president, I discovered the "double handshake" phenomenon. If I were simply introduced at a social gathering or on the street by my name, people quickly shook my hand. However, if, as often happened, I was further introduced as the president of such-and-such institution, people gripped my hand a second time and shook it more vigorously. In a sheer fraction of a moment, I had lost some of my personhood and became a symbol, worthy of attention not because of who I was but whom I represented. In terms of the general public, this action often reflected honor for the office or institution, but in academic circles it often meant I was valued more for what I might be able to do to assist them. I learned how flattery works and how subtlety distorts life. When I was on or near my campus, my ideas seemed insightful and my witty jokes were well received. However, in other settings, they seemed to lose their intellectual efficacy or humor!

Years ago I was warned by an ex-president of Willamette University about how fragile friendships are in academia. He told me that after many years of productive service he retired, only to discover that literally the next week people who he thought were his friends quit calling, trustees and others who had always wanted to play tennis were no longer available, and suddenly all those people who had wanted to share lunch seemingly had busy schedules unavailable to him.

I tried to prepare myself for that eventual reality, but until it happens to you one cannot really believe how many people relate to you for professional and business purposes only. When your status, power, or influence changes, your urgent phone calls diminish, e-mail invitations lessen, and seeming "friendships" vanish. If life is based on these transitory ties, then personal feelings of value and worth are challenged. It is at key moments like these that one realizes anew who the people are who love and care for you as a person while others see you only as means to an end they envision.

Are life's relationships and friendships better or worse in the local church? What has been your experience, Kent?

MILLARD: Don, your comments remind me of a statement in Proverbs 18:24, which in essence says: "There are friends who pretend to be friends and then there are true friends who stick closer than a brother."

I suspect that all of us have known people who pretended to be friends because they wanted something from us. As a pastor in a local congregation I have also had the experience of having people feign friendship to build up their ego and to gain knowledge about our family or about the church that they could use to boost their influence and importance in the congregation. I discovered that these persons would sometimes distort what I had said privately and undermine my leadership and credibility with others.

However, most of my experiences in the church have been with true friends who genuinely cared about us and were people with whom we could share deeply and honestly about our joys and sorrows, our victories and defeats. In the forty years since my ordination, we have served in seven different communities, and in every place have found dear and loving persons who remain friends to this day.

Even though we have usually lived and served in different communities sometimes hundreds of miles apart, whenever we talk on the phone or see each other personally it is as if we pick up from where we last talked—time and space seem to evaporate. Having a long-term friend like you has enabled me to discern when a person is pretending to be a friend and when he or she is a true friend "who walks in when the rest of the world walks out."

MESSER: Recognition of people's mixed motives for friendships, however, can lead to a paralysis of paranoia, where one questions every person's intentions and authenticity. Friendship, therefore, requires a level of risk-taking that can be mutually beneficial or prove to be disappointing or even destructive.

I remember that when I became president of Dakota Wesleyan University at the age of thirty, a seasoned dean told me not to make friends with faculty members, because your heart is sure to be broken. Tragically, he had taken his own advice over the years and did not seem to have any close friends in the small town of Mitchell, South Dakota. Bonnie and I decided we could not live the rest of our life that way, so we took the risk of becoming personal friends with faculty and others on the staff.

Clearly there was wisdom in the dean's advice, as sometimes relationships do get strained when there are differences in power, authority, and responsibility. But, fortunately, the positive good of making friends outweighed the negatives, and we have enjoyed lasting relationships over many decades. I cannot imagine how lonely administrative and public life can be without people whom you can trust—people who embrace you as a human being, warts and all.

MILLARD: It has been said that the essence of faith is risk and it is also true that the essence of friendship is risk. It seems to me that we have a choice about how we will live our lives. We can play our cards close to our chest, withhold ourselves from deeply investing in the lives of others, and refuse to ever be vulnerable with another person. We can choose to never get close to anyone because that is a way of protecting ourselves from ever being hurt.

However, if we never take the risk of being hurt we also never have the experience of deep joy. When we take the risk of becoming open, honest, and vulnerable with a friend we create the possibility of experiencing the joy of deep friendship and the satisfaction of life-giving relationships.

We have been appointed leaders in significant institutions of the church. Don, you served as president of higher education institutions for twenty years and I have served as senior pastor of a fifty-six-hundred-member United Methodist congregation for the past twelve years. Sometimes people say that it is lonely at the top, but I believe it is lonely only if we choose to make it so. As senior pastor of a large congregation I have experienced the friendship, support, guidance, and wisdom of a great leadership team so that I never felt that I had to make significant decisions alone. In fact, I believe that leadership is best expressed when we surround ourselves with trusted friends, colleagues and mentors.

THE MIRACLE OF FRIENDSHIP

MESSER: During my marathon presidencies, the average longevity of academic chief executives in the United States was about six years. Many a time I commented that I survived, and sometimes thrived, because of loyal friends and the grace of God. Of course, ultimately, you can only count on the grace of God. Sometimes even that seems distant, and we all are plunged into what the mystics call "the dark nights of the soul."

Surviving sudden downturns in life depends upon more than one friend, no matter how trusted and intense that relationship might be. For the last twenty-five years, for example, geographical distance has stretched our friendship, Kent, as neither of us truly could understand the context of our career struggles or the circumstances of the conflicts we endured. Thankfully, I have had other close friends, both male and female, of other races and nationalities, who have offered strength and support at key moments in life's journey. I started to name some of these special people and then realized I was so blessed with good friends that I ran the danger of forgetting to list some precious close friends who have stood beside me during the storms and stresses of life. Tragically, too often people in public life lack dependable friends who care about them as persons and/or couples.

Especially important for me has been the unique friendship that my wife and I have enjoyed with two other Colorado ministerial families, Paul and Paula Murphy, and John and Elaine Blinn. Colleagues in ministry but not career competitors, we men shared common values and hopes for the church and society, just as our spouses shared common interests in the professions of psychological counseling and social work. Friendship of this nature, of course, needs to be constantly cultivated, which we have accomplished by celebrating each other's birthdays, anniversaries, and special family events. For us, travel together in the United States and abroad has served to deepen our friendship and expand our horizons of common commitment. Thus when times of illness, death, career crisis, or whatever have inevitably struck one person or another, the rest of us were "there" during a time of crisis and beyond. Additionally, John and Paul, along with another pastoral colleague, Bill Selby, have provided me a unique support group for the past twenty years.

We have discovered that losing a friend through death is a really painful experience. There used to be three of us buddies, Kent, but suddenly melanoma cancer wiped out Darrel Leach. Somehow I even felt guilty that he got sick and died rather than me. After all, Darrel lived the more reasonable and healthier life, with less stress and more exercise. A more loyal and loving friend is hard to imagine, but his life was cut dramatically short. Surreal as it seems, he and I planned his funeral service between innings of a Colorado Rockies baseball game. I cannot fathom losing any more friends, but I know it is inevitable. It is a lesson of life that I do not look forward to learning.

MILLARD: Yes, the three of us were inseparable during our college days. After seminary we all served in United Methodist churches and institutions in South Dakota for about fifteen years. Every year we would get together with our families and celebrate New Year's Eve someplace in the state. Our spouses became best friends and our children grew up together, and even to this day our children are friends with each other. Perhaps when adults model real friendships together their children witness the value of having close friends and they grow up to develop deep and lasting friendships themselves.

Minnietta and I have two grown children who are both married and we have seven grandchildren. We are blessed because our children live in Indianapolis so we talk to them daily and spend some time each week with our grandchildren.

We have discovered a new dimension to friendship as we have become good friends with our grown children. Our son, Kendall, is an attorney and we talk regularly about work, family, faith, and politics, and we occasionally spend a day canoeing together. Our daughter, Koretta, is a social worker and we regularly attend sporting events with her and her children and have worked on community projects together. It seems to me to be a miracle that our children have grown to become two of our best friends.

THE MAKING OF FRIENDSHIPS

MESSER: Yes, what a blessing it is to have the intimate friendship of a spouse and one's adult children. Bonnie, Christine, and Kent have offered me unconditional love over the years, for which I am intensely grateful.

Several scientific studies have suggested that people with closer friends tend to have fewer ailments and even live up to 2.5 years longer. Not having friends might even be as harmful to one's health as obesity or smoking. Yet relatively few "how-to" books exist in regard to making and keeping friends. Those that have been written often focus on coping after losing a friend or were written for teenagers.

Therefore, I was interested in learning from a newspaper article that a woman in my home city of Denver, Veronica Montoya, is writing a book that will contain a "code of ethics" for friends. Apparently her book will focus on friendships among women, but three of her guidelines captured my attention, as I think they are not gender-specific.

First, you have to be a friend if you want to have a friend! Friendship is a two-way street, and this is simply another way of restating the Golden Rule. Secondly, Montoya, emphasizes that friends listen to one another, respect each other's time and talents, and overcome jealousies. "Envy," she says, "has to end for a friendship to be strong. Your friends are always going to have something you covet." Third, she emphasizes being nonjudgmental. The latter destroys relationships, she says, noting that "You may not agree with everything they do, but if they are a good friend, you shouldn't make your love conditional."

This reminds me of what I learned when I read the biography of Supreme Court Justice Harry Blackmun. A fascinating insight into the man who wrote the landmark Roe v. Wade abortion decision, the sad part of the story was how his lifelong friendship with Chief Justice Warren Burger disintegrated as they worked side by side. Once known as the "Minnesota Twins" because of their deep friendship and similar backgrounds in Minnesota, *Becoming Justice Blackmun* recounts how that friendship fractured as they gradually took opposing positions on critical judicial cases.[2]

Most friends at some point have conflicts, and dealing openly and honestly is recommended. Perhaps I am just naïve or suffer a poor memory, but I cannot think of a time in our fifty years of friendship that we have ever been in conflict or our friendship endangered. Correct me, please, or help me to understand how this could have been the case. Perhaps we are both too optimistic and idealistic or simply have chosen to avoid dealing with conflicts in our personal relationships.

MILLARD: Don, I have also wondered why we have never had a serious disagreement during our fifty years of friendship. We have had so many long conversations on every conceivable topic for so many years, I suspect each of us knows how the other would think and respond to any particular situation. Perhaps it is because we have such common backgrounds, education, and commitments that we think so much alike.

We both grew up in very small towns in South Dakota, we both attended the United Methodist Church and church camps together, majored in the same subjects at the same United Methodist college, were debate partners, played football together in college, and double dated. We went to the same seminary and developed similar theological attitudes toward life.

You felt called to serve God through serving as a college and seminary president and to extend your influence through teaching and the publication of many books. I felt called to serve God through serving as pastor of a local congregation and sought the transformation of the world through the mission and outreach of a local church and the publication of a few books.

While we serve in different settings, our goal and vision is to be used by God to transform our world into a compassionate, just, inclusive, and Christlike community; so perhaps our common vision has overshadowed everything else, including disagreements.

THE MINISTRY OF FRIENDSHIP

MESSER: Friends have been called by psychologists our "family by choice." Neither of us had a brother, so, in essence, we found one! "De facto families" of friends often provide us a more homogeneous and compatible family than the one we inherited.

Sometimes I think God created families so we could not hide from the diversity of human experiences and viewpoints in the world—at holiday dinners we have to listen to a political perspective or social commentary foreign to our own ideas and ideology. Many times family connections are maintained out of a sense of obligation, not genuine affection.

Most people need and choose friends because we share similar values and commitments. Frankly it is easier for me to be with a Jewish or Buddhist friend than a right-wing or fundamentalist Christian of my own denomination. Some years ago when I tried to stimulate formal dialogues between so-called liberals and evangelicals in the United Methodist Church, I found it exceptionally difficult. To be truthful, most don't even like each other, much less love one another!

This conflicts directly with the teachings of Jesus who calls us to "love one another as I have loved you. No one has greater love than this, to lay down one's life for one's friends" (John 15:12–13). The presumption of Christianity is that Jesus' followers will be friends. Like the words on a t-shirt that I saw a boy wearing in Argentina, we are called to be "amigos por Jesus." We have been appointed disciples, "friends for Jesus," so we can be apostles reaching out to the world in care and compassion. "Holy friendships" should be the norm of Christian life, not the exception.

MILLARD: It seems to me that friendship is as much an action as it is a feeling. It is not enough to say "friend, friend" if we do not demonstrate friendship by our actions.

Don, you have demonstrated friendship to me in countless ways. Twelve years ago Bishop Woodie White called me and asked if I would consider coming to Indianapolis to serve St. Luke's United Methodist Church following Dr. Carver McGriff, who had served the congregation for twenty-six years, built the congregation from one hundred to four thousand members, and was retiring and staying in the community.

After I received the call from Bishop White, I first called my wife and then I called you to seek guidance and discernment about this invitation to move to a new conference and state and follow a long-term, highly effective pastor.

As usual, you asked the right questions for me to ponder and it was always clear that you would support whatever decision I made. I don't know how I could have ever made such a dramatic and life changing decision without the love, support, and encouragement of you and my loving wife, Minnietta.

MESSER: Kent, do you have a theology of friendship that you share with your congregation? It seems to me that Christianity offers a radical alternative to those who envision God as always almighty and omnipotent. The idea of Emmanuel, God with us, and an immanent God available to every person suggests a "holy friendship" that would be unthinkable and even sacrilegious in some religious traditions.

Personally, I find great consolation and hope in the traditional hymn, "What a Friend We Have in Jesus." How daring for Christians to claim a friendship with Jesus, the Christ, the second person of the Trinity! Yet we sing boldly, "What a friend we have in Jesus, all our sins and griefs to bear!" and "Can we find a friend so faithful who will all our sorrows share?"

Human friendships at their best, like that relationship we have shared over many decades, I believe, are a good but imperfect glimpse of the Divine—a taste of God's great future for all of us.

MILLARD: In John's Gospel Jesus tells his disciples that the best description of his relationship with them is that of "friends." Jesus says: "I do not call you servants any longer, because the servant does not know what the master is doing; but I have called you friends . . ." (John 15:15).

Throughout the Gospels, the relationship between Jesus and his followers was described as that of teacher and disciples or master and servants. However, as Jesus comes to the end of his life he gives his followers a new and more important title: he calls them " friends" as if to say that the highest and best relationship he could have with them is that of friendship.

In friendship there is no hierarchy in the relationship. One is not over the other as teacher, master, boss, or leader. In real friendship there is a beautiful equality of relationship where each one is valued for who he or she is, accepted warts and all, and cherished for his or her love and commitment. It is amazing to me that Jesus came to the point in his life that he called his followers "friends," and perhaps when we see Jesus as a good and faithful friend we will trust him and love him even more.

We have been through every phase of life together: dating girls (sometimes the same girl at different times), getting married, raising children, getting an education, traveling overseas together, working together on common church projects, and supporting the same political candidates.

Now we are both moving into a new phase of life as we look toward the redeployment of our time and energy for the broader community rather than just one particular institution. I suspect that we will continue the late-night phone calls and the e-mail messages as we work together to help end hunger now and make the world AIDS-free and develop meaningful relationships across national and religious lines.

When I look back over my life I realize that my life has been significantly shaped by three friends. I became genuinely acquainted with all three of them at a church camp in South Dakota nearly fifty years ago. In 1958 I attended Lake Poinsett Methodist Camp in eastern South Dakota and the week I was there I met Jesus Christ in a personal way; I met Minnietta Green, who later became my wife; and I met you, my closest lifelong friend. I thank God for the gift of all three of these friends.

In Closing: God's gift of a friendship like ours is what we would wish for every person during his or her journey of life. Through heartbreaks and hopes, trials and triumphs, sadness and success, life is enriched and enhanced by friendships that not only bond two people together but create networks of meaningful relationships of support and care. In our daily living, we get a glimpse of divine joy.

Notes

1. Judith Viorst, *Necessary Losses* (New York: Simon and Schuster, 1986).

2. Linda Greenhouse, *Becoming Justice Blackmun: Harry Blackmun's Supreme Court Journey* (New York: Times Books, 2005).

TWELVE

SO WHAT IF MY BEST FRIEND IS A RIVER?

DONNA SCHAPER

My best friend is the Hudson River. I see her blue or grey, dark or clear, seasoned or seasonless. We have been best friends since I was a kid growing up on the wrong side of town in Kingston, New York. I ice skated on Dinky's pond, a tributary to the great river, and sometimes if the water was cold enough long enough, without snow, I could skate a twig-cluttered finger all the way to a river view. The pond was the threshold for the river. It thrilled me to see her snaking there, southing to the big city. I never see her without that girlish thrill, even today from Manhattan's East Village where 1.4 miles later I can be close to tugs and barges, hawks and shad, rivers emptying into the big sea.

Winter was just the appetizer for the summer. Then, I moved "downtown" to the Point, the name we who had not much else called our river spa. There I swam and swam and swam some more. When I got done swimming, I would swim some more. Eventually some intrusive adult would scoop me up, dry me off, and take me to a place they called home but I did not. The Hudson received me without comment. She accepted me, skinny butt and all. Now she accepts me with the fat one. In other words, she is still my friend fifty-eight years later.

I bring her up in this essay on friendship although I do have other friends. They are not so faithful or accepting but they are still my friends. Two have already died. If I spoke the truth, I would say they died on me. When it comes to friendship, selfishness often prevails. Judith swam with me in the river. Her mother did not like my mother and thought Judith was slumming when she was with me. Judith did not, which is what made our make believe so precious. I could sit with her under the hedge and escape her mother's judging eyes and my mother's shamed ones. We lived next door. There between the lots we could make believe there was no such thing as class or a future that needed our mobility upward. There we could play—and surely the first thing a friend needs to be is a playmate. Judith died on the New York State Thruway in a snowstorm on her way back from college at Thanksgiving. The lights never went back on in her mother's eyes. Not even the judgment remained. Just blanks. How could this have happened to someone with so much promise, so much forward thrust, so much expectation pressuring her onward and upward? My grief was not about the lost future: Judith's death meant hedge and make believe were gone. There were fewer safe places to hide. She took a piece of play with her. I still had the river. When I heard about her death, I too was in college. I drove to Kingston, went to the Point, and wept. The river did not notice how small my tears were to its water. It was not an uncaring not noticing. It was something different, something about grief, loss, and proportion. Like that boat being so small and the sea being so wide. She was particularly beautiful that day, ice starting to heave like my chest.

Before Judith I had already lost Sue. She was the catcher and I was the pitcher on the South Carolina state champion girl's softball team. Our partnership won the final game. Sue hit with vigor and I pitched with accuracy if not speed. I nicked the corners if she told me which one to nick. She caught my balls; she even caught the bad throws. She rarely missed one and if one got away, she would kill herself going after it. Sue did not care if she got hurt. We were thirteen and the kind of girls who lit up rooms with the effervescence we had for and with each other. We laughed at our own jokes. We giggled and slept close at sleepovers, sat together on the team bus and understood just enough about the other to be able to roll eyes at our parents and other team members in tandem. What Sue and I had can only be called rhythm. I know they say white people don't have rhythm but that is wrong. Good friends have rhythm. We have an internal metronome and it speaks to the other ones so that we can keep moving while being really steady. The second thing about good friends is that they are polyrhythmic. We remain totally ourselves—even become more of ourselves when we are with our friends—because we beat to each other's drum, keeping all and letting all go at the same time.

My family had left Kingston when I was eleven. I had not seen my river for two years when Sue died of a sudden onslaught brain tumor that first crippled and then killed her. Seeing her not being able to move was one of the hardest things of my entire life. When she died, I was relieved. I did not want to see her like that any more. She had been so agile, so flexible, so strong, and so quick. Now she was out of rhythm with her own nervous system. I also wanted to go to the river but could not. It was too far. But I had memories of what it was like in late spring: swollen, angry, running fast, ice banging into ice making loud noises in an otherwise silent place. Ice cracked and heaved on the edges, sometimes with a bang, other times with a hoarse crackle. My grief was the hoarse crackle and the fast running fluid of tears. I was way too young to know this much about friendship. When Judith died I feared I would go hoarse and hurt again. I did not. I was prepared by the way life oddly went on after Sue died. We played ball the next year. We did not win but we played. Something in the river's permanence had put me on to this thing about going on and on. "Deep River" is the spiritual. "Just keeps rolling, rolling, rolling along."

These early griefs (and a few thousand others) turned me into a person who was not very good at friendship. I was popular all right, but not much of a friend. I kept myself for the river, not just the Hudson but any river; I kept myself to myself and relied more on nature than humans, more on me than "them," more on inner than outer. I think that is a choice many people make. People are just not reliable. Rivers are. My first marriage was to my then best friend. But it turned out that he did not have much to say. I still love him (our fortieth anniversary would be in 2008), but we stopped being the kind of friends you can be with a river. There was so much of me he did not want to receive. I was to keep the talkative part over there. I was to keep the ambitious part in another closet. I was to be happier, by which he meant content on the farm. We had a great farm! But contentment did not issue from it for me the way it issued for him. Friends enjoy the same thing; unfriends do not.

For twenty-five years we had Thanksgiving with the same four couples. We were all rooted in a college, Gettysburg in Pennsylvania, whose apple orchards had given us the same joy rivers can. We had lived large and outside, picked blackberries and made jelly together, told each other everything and more, stayed up all night, baptized each other's children, and are now attending their weddings. On Thanksgiving we competed to cook, fought about the right temperature for the turkey and how long it should roast—while the sensible ones of us took off down by the oldest apple tree and gazed up at the house lighting up to challenge November's early night. "The idiosyncratic eloquence of an old twisted apple tree, weighed down by the fruit it has born," said someone wise about apple trees, who could have been talking about our Thanksgiving table. Six of the eight are with new partners. One of those partners took the other out of the group, and then we were six. Someone (me) mentioned his ex and his un-ex went to the bathroom and stayed there for the entire meal. Of the six remaining at year twenty-five of listening to Arlo Guthrie sing "Alice's Restaurant" before sitting to feast, two are now bitterly divorced. Neither chooses to come alone or with their new friends. The other two climbed down into the dark cellar of late stage alcoholism, with the healthier one dying last year, leaving the more ill one alone with her two sons for me to care for. With friends like this, who needs enemies? The last five years involved the near erasure of the good times, especially when one took the butternut squash soup and spilled it, steaming, all over the groaning table just as the meal was to be eaten. Why? She was drunk. That's why. At fifty-eight I have made a promise not to make any new friends until I take better care of the ones I have. (Of course, the day I made that promise to myself, I met a woman whom I really like and we enjoy each other's writing in many ways.)

One of the women left from the group of eight remains my best friend. I do not even speak to the other. On January 1, 2000, we all gathered at a retreat center in the Poconos with about forty other folk of the extended family and communal network. My former friend had been in alcohol rehab for a month. She came out for the party. At breakfast she sat at the table, on the first day of the millennium, drinking rum. The one remaining friend and I tried to stop her. We also cleaned up her poop in a bed on the day of her husband's funeral—her organs have started to go. But my cohort in poop and funerals, we see each other a lot. She lives uptown and I live downtown where the river meets the sea. We play often. We hide in hedges and giggle. Sometimes we pitch and catch. We go over painful memories and joyous ones, interchangeably. We e-mail constantly. I could not love her more nor want her happiness to be increased any more.

I have spent way too many hours thinking about this multilayered Thanksgiving tragedy. My second husband, who became part of this group and actually became its center twenty years ago, and I have decided we cannot talk about it or them any more. Enough said. Too painful. We will stick with their children but that's about it. We will have less expansive Thanksgivings. We will play "Alice's Restaurant" and remember to pick up the garbage. Our only strategy is to make younger friends and see what happens. So far, so bad. There are no memories to discuss. The present is boring compared to a past.

Friendship is not friendship if it is not interesting. Friendship is playful when it is good. Friendship is rhythmic when it is good. And friendship is terribly painful when it is not playful or rhythmic.

Speaking of my second husband, he also is my best friend. He is the only person who understands me. And he does not completely get it or me. He is more rhythmic than playful but then again he is not a girl. But he gets so close so often, and that and the fact that we have all those photo albums and spilled soups to share means that I am insanely dependent on him. If he goes before me, I will be nothing but bereft. But as I said before, I do have other friends. The Hudson will not leave before I do and that is an important piece of this friendship business.

When it comes to friendship, I have a very small budget. And I have to save for my retirement. These friendship frugalities and fears (I really do not want to get hurt again) are inconsequential to the Hudson River. The keep rolling thing is all that is on her mind.

Why is the Hudson River my best friend? Because she will not predecease me. I told you friendship is selfish. I should also have admitted that it is self-protective. The Hudson is playful and in her I can play. Because of all the Pete Seegers of the world, we can swim in her again. Mercifully, I was in the South when the worst pollution happened. I did go to Kingston once and saw what had happened to Dinky's and the Point. Horrifying. It was like somebody went alcoholic on the river and polluted and poisoned it. It was yellow and green instead of blue and grey. Finally I think the river is my best friend because of its longer, deeper wider, life rhythms. I am way too dependent on Warren. I think he is life to and for me. He is not. There is a bigger thing called life and I swim in it.

THIRTEEN

THE RIVER FLOWING BENEATH THE WORDS

Still Learning How to Be a Friend

KAREN STONE

Why am I writing about friendship?

If you are looking for a friend—someone to listen to you, be there for you whenever you're down, sense your mood, call or write frequently, share with you, establish and nourish a spiritual connection—I might not be your first choice. I am not the best friend or at least not the most attentive of friends. Stubbornly self-reliant, I often am content to be alone, even when anyone could see that I really need others. (Like the time Howard, my husband, had major surgery and I sat alone in the waiting room, pretending to be brave as the hours went by, more hours than it should have taken. Why didn't I ask someone to sit with me? I was an emotional wreck when it was over.)

Oh, I have had good friends over the years. Have them.

Childhood friends—there must have been several, but Cheryl is the one I remember best. I recollect sleepovers, games of twenty questions, a bat loose in her parents' big, rambling house by Medicine Lake. (Once, when we were about twelve, a sudden, fierce thunderstorm caught us out rowing on the lake; terrified, we prayed together out loud as we leaned into the oars and fought our way to shore.) When my family moved to California, I lost touch with her. Didn't write. Even now, decades later, I think about her often but still don't call or write. Half of every year I live within 225 miles of her, but do I stop to visit? No, I do not.

Teenage friends—Osa, Annette, Deirdre. I walked both ways to Van Nuys High School with Osa every day, Osa the actor with the long auburn hair and the odd laugh. Osa was comfortable, a little klutzy, and creative; she brought out a dramatic flair in me. There were sleepovers with Annette the surfer at her family's beach house, laughing, flirting with boys I did not know and would not see again, spreading avocados from their tree on crisp toast for breakfast. Annette was pure fun; she helped me let my hair down and enjoy each moment to the fullest. And there were long philosophical talks with Deirdre the intellectual, avant-garde Deirdre, experimenting with ideas, attending Young Democrats meetings in smoke-filled L.A. basements. Deirdre was stimulating; she helped me raise the bar, widen my view, expect more of myself.

Then I graduated and moved away, lost touch with all of them.

Next came Howard, right after high school, my one friend for life. We are as different as night and day, but he is the friend who listens to me with intensity. Who tells me hard truths. Who loves me no matter what I do, no matter how much my higgledy-piggledy approach to living distresses him. Who a few years back told me, as we strolled down a shaded street in a picturesque South African town, that if he ever got really mad at me and died of a heart attack in the midst of his anger, I should remember that he loves me dearly. That I must recall this conversation. (Writing of this gift that he gave me brings fresh tears to my eyes.) Howard is also the one to whom I listen—interrupt more than I should, but still listen. Just now, as I was writing, he walked into the room to tell me about something he had bought for his vintage radio collection and I thought, "He's interrupting my train of thought," and then "No, he wants to tell me this." I stopped to listen.

So, Howard. And thus began a long stretch (forty-four years and counting) of couple friends and only a few that were just mine.

Seminary years (his)—we had couple friends and I had Marian, my coworker at *The Lutheran* magazine in Philadelphia. We shared daily lunch and coffee break conversation, parties and meals at her suburban house, and a sense of family when I was young and living far from parents and siblings. Marian was an important friend at a difficult time in my life, though I probably never told her so. Then we moved away, and I lost touch with Marian. She was nearly my mother's age and Mom's been gone for six years; I do not even know if Marian is still alive.

Graduate school years (his)—couple friendships, good ones, but there was no one at work I could call a friend. Moved again.

Graduate school years (mine)—we had one really close couple friendship at church—the "Bob" half of which has survived to this day, one of those great lifelong friendships that you can pick up after a long lapse as if no time at all had intervened. But graduate school should be a natural time to form lasting personal relationships, and I cannot remember the name of a single student colleague from those years. My one friend was Muriel, my art professor and mentor. We spent long hours together, conversing over pots of coffee at a university café, working on collaborative art projects, attending consciousness-raising meetings. At one of those meetings Muriel announced, "We always hear women say that their husbands are their best friends, but I've just realized that my best friend is Karen." I was nonplussed. Could I say the same? Certainly she was my best friend after Howard, but . . . maybe the mentor relationship is easier for the mentor than it is for the student. Later, when we moved from Arizona to Texas, I lost touch with her as well—didn't call, didn't write, let it slide.

You can see the pattern: getting friends, even tending the friendships when we were thrown together by circumstance or work, but sooner or later (when a job change or distance intervened) letting the relationships wither for lack of nourishment.

And then there was LoreRetta. She was my friend apart—away from the university, away from church, away from the college where I later taught, away, in fact, from much of my experience. I met her at her husband's auto wrecking yard when Howard and I were just starting a four-year-long escapade with stock car racing (that's another story). Her eyes sparkled. She had a quick wit, a sharp tongue, a fully charged personality. I was smitten.

This was one friendship I did not let slide. She did not give me a chance. Only a few years later and just months after moving away, we were back in Arizona, sitting on undertakers' folding chairs under an awning shading us from the relentless desert sun, saying goodbye.

For a few short years I considered LoreRetta my best friend. Was I hers? Perhaps at the beginning. It was hard to know because of my relative inexperience at building and tending friendships. I never asked her outright. But she was also part of a couple relationship so we saw each other often—every Friday night during racing season at the very least.

We could talk for hours when we were together. But the world in which our friendship grew was male-centered, to put it mildly. Usually women were the supporters, the cheerleaders and parts runners, in some cases sex objects. You might think that would create a special bond between the women, and sometimes it did, but we always knew the men would come first not only on the race track or in the pits, but in our friendship.

When her husband got a racing sponsor whose wife was about our age, LoreRetta shifted focus from me to Jill. I became invisible. In a group, they would talk without a glance at me. In a restaurant they would head for the ladies' room without asking me to join them. It was almost like being back in junior high school; I felt unfamiliar twinges of hurt feelings but acted as if it was nothing. Trying to be the grown up, I rushed to protect myself with a shell of cool maturity. Did I bring up the subject with LoreRetta? Certainly not. Even if my nonconfrontational temperament would have allowed it, I judged that the conversation would have been embarrassing for her. When Jill was not around, it was as if nothing had changed. When LoreRetta got sick, Jill disappeared.

There was something fragile about LoreRetta, in spite of her spunk and her tough talk. She'd had a lot of illness in the past, and now lived with lupus. She told her husband she had given up smoking, but the truth was she did not ever quit. I would sit in the bathroom with her, the fan running loudly, while she sneaked a quick cigarette. At least this kept the numbers down.

Then Howard and I moved again. It was exciting, but this time we had put down roots and found it harder to leave. For once I stayed in touch with an absent friend, telephoned, wrote quick notes in the months after we went away. Then came the letter, eight or nine pages in LoreRetta's round script. Reading it, I pictured in my mind the many times—watching a race from the pits, standing in the kitchen, talking and laughing while the men worked on a car—when I had noticed a quick movement of her hand to the middle of her chest. It was not just a mannerism. The little pang was not pleurisy, as she had once insisted. Now she wrote that the lung cancer was so far advanced by the time they opened her chest that "they just sewed me back up again."

I flew back, spent a week with her during radiation treatments, plied her with milkshakes and cheesecake to get her weight up. We talked of radiation, hospitals, doctors, but mostly about the things we had always talked about. We said "I love you" but casually, the way friends do. Didn't talk about dying. Didn't say good-bye forever, just good-bye for now. It seemed perfunctory, but that was our style. We could hear the river of emotion flowing beneath our words. When I got on the plane to go back home, I knew I would never see her again.

In a few weeks we were back again, sitting at the graveside of this friend I had loved. Hearing the Twenty-third Psalm, recognizing restrained emotion in a glance, a touch, a faraway look. Shaking hands with good people in their best clothes, their shapes and colors distorted through my tears. Back at the house, I cooked and served with the other women as LoreRetta (and Martha) would have done, while her husband and the other men stayed out in the driveway shooting baskets until it was too dark to see.

I did not abandon her; she abandoned me.

This was not the sort of relationship you might think of when you hear the term "spiritual friendship." We did not talk about faith and our conversations were seldom what you would consider deep. Those things were understood rather than spoken. Probably I talked a lot; I usually do. Perhaps if I had spent more time listening to LoreRetta I would have known her better, offered more and received more in the friendship. But it was an important step for me. In spite of the limitations posed by our very different subcultures and a mutual reticence to share our feelings for each other directly, we did speak with (for me) astonishing openness about our lives and our relationships. I jumped into the friendship feet first, with uncharacteristic abandon, thus opening myself to hurt feelings (when LoreRetta appeared to lose interest in me) and grief (when she left us all).

Today I have a few fine friends. I still talk too much, but when I remember to listen I am rewarded with insight into another person's unique gifts. There is Lynn, for one, who in some ways is remarkably like my old friend LoreRetta—definitely an individual, quirky and proud of it, unlike anyone else you will meet. We create fantastic meals for each other, not competitively but with full appreciation for the other's style in the kitchen and with the tacit understanding that each meal is a loving gift. We talk about what good friends we are, but do not get too emotional or touchy-feely. It's not our way. We are fierce competitors over a Scrabble board, giving and receiving no quarter but enjoying every moment. Lynn is unchurched and always has been, as far as I know. But because she is curious about me, she asks some fresh and unexpected questions that have contributed to my spiritual growth because they made me express in words my experience of faith and doubt.

Up to now Lynn has been a summer friend; come August I return south to my workday world. When I leave, she will not say good-bye. During the school year we do not see each other and tend to talk only when our husbands have been chatting with each other and pass the phone to us. She usually sends one or two long, funny, expressive letters over the winter, but I almost never write.

This traipsing back and forth between Minnesota and Texas makes it harder to have close friendships. We are not alone in that; this is an age of high mobility and interrupted relationships. In these circumstances friendship is not as easy as it is for next-door neighbors who have known each other since third grade. I could stand to get better at being a friend even when separated, to find the extra few minutes it takes to pick up a phone and call, to send the card or e-mail or small gift that says, "You're still on my mind; I haven't forgotten you; soon we'll pick up where we left off."

When I am working, I seem to limit the scope and length and depth of my friendships. I care for my students and tend them in many ways, but there are at least a thousand of them and they move on out of my life quickly. I teach at three schools, which only encourages my tendency toward self-reliance; between bites of food on a thirty-minute lunchtime I can have a great conversation with a colleague I really like, then it's "Ciao, see you next week." I offer hospitality and sometimes declare my love to a few good friends but do not see any of them daily or even weekly. Like Martha, friend of Jesus, I am worried and distracted by many things. I do not put in the time that I imagine a spiritually nourishing friendship requires.

I do love the Luke account of Martha and Mary. (I am especially sympathetic toward Martha.) In fact, on one of the few times I have offered a sermon as a lay preacher, that was my text. Perhaps I am so interested in Mary and Martha because I am a woman, and I am working on friendship issues in my own life, and here are two strong women who were good friends of Jesus long before the description of their encounters in Luke:

> Now as they went on their way, [Jesus] entered a certain
> village, where a woman named Martha welcomed him

into her home. She had a sister named Mary, who sat at the Lord's feet and listened to what he was saying. But Martha was distracted by her many tasks; so she came to him and asked, "Lord, do you not care that my sister has left me to do all the work by myself? Tell her then to help me." But the Lord answered her, "Martha, Martha, you are worried and distracted by many things; there is need of only one thing. Mary has chosen the better part, which will not be taken away from her. (Luke 10:38–42)

As a child growing up in a Lutheran parsonage, I was more of a Mary than a Martha. Our father encouraged us to sit in on theological discussions (while presumably our mother was in the kitchen, Thelma being Martha). Those conversations had a role in shaping me, shaping the way I do theology, shaping my faith.

As an adult, I appear to have become more of a Martha. I am the one who cooks the gourmet meal and prepares the appetizers, makes up the bed with clean smooth sheets, sets out matching towels, and does whatever household tasks are needed to prepare for a guest. Busy in the kitchen, I often have missed out on long stretches of rich conversation.

In the Luke story, Jesus seems to have prized what Mary did more than what Martha did. But this is only one anecdote, one moment in a long-term friendship. In John's account, Martha was the assertive believer, the one who ran out to Jesus when he arrived four days after their brother Lazarus had died. She did not demand a miracle from Jesus, but avowed that even now God would grant whatever Jesus might ask. She confessed: "I believe that you are the Messiah, the Son of God, the one coming into the world" (John 11:27). Mary came out to Jesus only after her sister called her, then fell to his feet and seemed to reproach him for not arriving sooner, otherwise Lazarus would not have died. Jesus' close relationship with this family group is evident in the emotional scene that followed, with many (including Jesus) weeping in their grief over the death of this well-loved man.

Both Mary and Martha were courageous and steadfast friends. They took great risks to befriend Jesus, to offer him their hospitality, to declare and demonstrate their love and faith at this dangerous time. The religious authorities were after him; he was a wanted man. In spite of the danger, with Lazarus alive and recovered, they again hosted Jesus in their home. On this occasion, according to John, Martha tended and served while Mary once again sat at his feet, this time pouring a very expensive and fragrant ointment on his feet and then drying them with her hair. It seems to me an almost reckless act of consuming love.

In the Luke story, Jesus did not disparage Martha's tangible, less ardent contributions. I have heard preachers say that he rebuked her, but if so it was a very gentle rebuke, more of a loving admonishment. He repeated her name affectionately: "Martha, Martha, you are worried and distracted by many things." There is no evidence that he had anything but appreciation for the food well prepared, the comfortable room, and the occasion to relax and be himself.

What did Mary do that brought on Martha's complaint and Jesus' approval? She listened to what he was saying. And what was he saying? I have always assumed he was teaching a group of men and that Mary's presence was tolerated much as we children were indulged when we sat in on theological conversations in our home. But Luke does not tell us what the Lord was saying, and maybe it does not matter. Maybe we are not supposed to know. He might have been teaching a group of guests, but it is also possible this was only a conversation between Mary and Jesus. Whatever it was he had to say that evening—whether he shared his wisdom or spilled out his frustrations, joys, or fears (for Jesus, fully human, might well have needed to share these human emotions)—Mary listened to what he was saying. I think that is what Jesus meant when he said that Mary had "chosen the better part." On this occasion, while Martha attended to Jesus' physical needs for a safe haven, a good meal, and a comfortable place to rest (and did so at great personal risk), Mary listened to Jesus and thereby attended to her own spiritual needs.

A talker and a busy-bee who often is distracted by many things, I need to remember this story often. Listening, being really curious, wanting to know about the other, is one of the key elements of friendship. I think especially about suppertime each evening in our home. Howard, my true friend, sits down at the table with me. We exchange stories. We describe our day. We talk about events and opinions, personalities and ideas, successes and frustrations. Most important, we listen to each other. It feels good to tell, but telling is not enough; we each need someone who will listen to the tale. When Howard is away, I miss the chance at the end of the day to talk but also to be heard.

This is true not only in my marriage but also with close friends—even those whom I see only every so many years. In spite of time elapsed, these friendships seem to continue uninterrupted. We bring each other up to date with what has happened in our families and in our lives. We listen to each other and are listened to.

Telling stories to someone who does not fully listen soon dissipates whatever joys came with the telling. The important thing in a conversation between friends is that someone who cares for you, appreciates you, and shares some history with you really hears what you have to say. Adds to it, perhaps, corrects or even argues with it, okay, but hears it.

It is equally important not only to be heard but also to listen, for in hearing we not only gain understanding of the other; we receive treasures (I remind myself) that are unavailable to the self-obsessed talker. The treasures we receive probably have more to do with the process—the curiosity, the caring and attending—than with the actual words that are spoken.

Listening is what Mary offered to Jesus. Perhaps Martha listened, too, when she finished her work and took off her apron. I do not think this story from scripture is telling me not to be a Martha. Both Mary and Martha are held up as loyal, loving friends of Jesus. Martha showed her love concretely, just as I often show my love to friends by cooking and serving them a good meal. Hospitality is essential to spiritual friendship. But hospitality does not only mean feeding our friends or setting out fresh towels for their comfort. Jesus said that Mary had chosen the better part. By listening to Jesus she offered him hospitality, and thereby received a spiritual gift that could not be taken away from her. Listening is a kind of hospitality of the heart that welcomes the speaker and enriches the listener.

Be a Martha if you will, the story says to me, but take a page from Mary's book. Slow down, do not be so distracted and worried. Listen. We may be talking about spiritual issues, or we may be talking about our hobbies or even the weather. The content is not as important as the telling and the listening, the time spent, the attention given that says I am curious about you, I am interested in you, I am with you.

I am learning to be a better friend. I will not always be so busy. Soon, perhaps, I will be able to work at my own pace, choosing when to work outside the home and when to be in my studio making art or writing, or in the garden gardening, or doing volunteer work, or taking long walks in the country, or having lunch and a gallery visit with a friend.

I am peering into the future and seeing my stubborn self-reliance as a potential problem in retirement, both physically and spiritually. To accompany me on the next stage of my spiritual journey I will need a few more good friends. Need a friend, be a friend, the saying goes. It would serve me well to look at times in the past when I did put in the time that friendship required, and then start doing more of it. Talk less and listen more.

At the same time, writing this has helped me see that there is more than one style of friendship. To be a better friend I will not need to transform my personality or morph into a different person. Looking back, I recognize the many times in my life when a friendship has spurred me to spiritual growth—to risk hurt, to feel the pain of loss and find meaning in it, to offer my presence, to answer tough questions, to face doubt and articulate what I believe. I also recognize that on those occasions when I really listened to a friend, and my friend really listened to me, it mattered little if we were talking about roses or redemption, politics or prayer, grandchildren or growth in the Spirit. We heard each other's words, and we heard the river flowing beneath the words.

I think that from time to time I have been a better friend than I knew.

FOURTEEN

CLOUD OF WITNESSES

MAREN C. TIRABASSI and MARIA I. TIRABASSI

When we received an invitation to write a chapter in this volume, we were pleased and excited. We have worked together on three books, and, for the last one, we were coauthors and co-editors. Nevertheless, it was a different kind of a challenge to respond as mother and daughter to the theme of friendship as it relates to our spirituality. We asked ourselves: Does friendship mean the same thing and have the same affect on faith, personal growth, and relationship to God for different generations?

The editors gave us clues. They offered seven or eight questions for us to explore as entrance points to the topic. We decided to choose four and respond to them independently, in hopes of demonstrating the similarities and differences between a fifty-four-year-old and a twenty-two-year-old.

We also decided on a format of telling stories about particular friends instead of theorizing. Storytelling worked for Jesus! The following are brief reflections about friends who affected the landscape of our spiritual journeys. They are preceded by the questions that inspired them and are signed by each of us. Our conclusion? We are not so different after all.

HOW HAS BETRAYAL BY FRIENDS AFFECTED ONE'S OWN SPIRITUAL LIFE?
It was New Year's Eve, freshman year of college, and I was going to a party with two of my best friends from high school. We were single and

reveling in it, and we made promises to each other that night that whatever happened, if one of us hooked up with a guy, the other two would stick together.

The party was small. When we arrived, it consisted only of us and two boys—one was my friend Miriam's ex-boyfriend, the other, his best friend. Miriam had confided to me while we were getting dressed that she had a little crush on her ex's best friend; on hearing this, our third friend, Lee, had asked Miriam if it was okay that she was interested in her ex.

I should have known before I set foot inside that this was a bad sign. Of the three of us, I had always been the voice of reason, and they were both in holiday spirits. At three A.M. though, when the second bedroom door closed and I was left alone on the couch, I was in shock. I could only think that I had left my shoes and coat in that bedroom, that I had promised to take Lee to work the next morning, that I could not, under any circumstances, force myself into the car and home. My parents' friends were sleeping in my bed. I had nowhere to go.

I sat on that couch all night. I kept putting movies on to drown out the sounds coming through thin walls. I took a walk and prayed that when I returned, one or both of them would have remembered our promises.

At 8:30 A.M., Lee was the first to come out. I stared at the television so that I would not cry in front of anyone. I drove them home, skipping a song on my favorite CD that mentioned a "Miriam." I dropped Lee off and it was the last time I ever saw her.

Miriam, on the other hand, kept calling. I could not talk to her for three days, but when I finally could, she listened to everything I told her and accepted it. She kept accepting it over the days and months that followed, continued to call even though I was still angry, and eventually, she broke through. I exhausted the hurt before she had finished asking for my forgiveness.

—*Maria*

I was lucky enough to be young the first time I was betrayed by a friend. Two times, two friends—two short stories.

I was a lonely only child—a little too smart, too plump, and my father's active alcoholism kept me from bringing friends home. There is an age when the most important thing in the world is to reciprocate a sleepover.

Three years after my dad's recovery, when our family was smiling again and I was in tenth grade, Carol became my friend. We did everything together—we read the same books, saw the same movies, played "Twister," snuck a friend's Ouija board into her bedroom, even doubledated. A liberal Presbyterian, I visited her strict Lutheran church. Carol and I knew what each other was thinking. And then one day, without warning, she passed a note in class saying she could not be my friend anymore.

My father suspected AA was not acceptable to her family—he was a bit of a crusader. I suspected that forays into wildness—more talk than action—made her uneasy. I never learned the reason or whether it came from Carol herself or her family. Someone who knew me inside and out consciously decided not to associate with me. It was far more shattering than any early difficulty making friends.

The other story? A friend asked me to the senior prom. Call him Harvey. A friend asked me to the senior prom—something I had never in my wildest fantasies expected to attend. A friend asked me to the senior prom because he knew I was not dating anyone . . . and then stood me up.

Thank you, Carol and Harvey. I could not have been more fragile than I was in those days. I did not break. And from then on, I knew that I would not break. The night of the senior prom a college boy I knew called to ask if I had seen the play in the basement of the Unitarian church—I took off my gown and slipped on jeans and loafers. Instead of causing me to mistrust friends, I discovered that imperfect friends cannot really damage me as long as I am intact inside. Friends can help, can nurture, can challenge, can give great joy, but when they harm I let them go.

—Maren

HOW HAVE FRIENDS GIVEN SPIRITUAL GUIDANCE DURING DIFFICULT TIMES?

This sort of event haunts ministers—we know it occurs sometimes and pray it will not happen to us.

Gary had a lifelong mental illness that responded to medication for years until a side-effect caused kidney problems. When he went into the hospital he was not critically ill, he was not elderly, he was simply having an episode of his illness. As I arrived the staff were putting him into solitary because his behavior disrupted a group. I let them lead me away and as I did, I heard him call out, "Pastor! Pastor!" The next day I went to the hospital to see a baby with spinal meningitis. Praying with the family left me emotionally drained. I decided not to visit Gary. He died in the night of heart failure.

Guilt overwhelmed me. I had trashed my ordination vows. Of course, I performed the funeral and the unwitting family was grateful. During a tormented year, I preached sermons, led Bible studies, attended meetings. I could neither forgive myself nor ask God for forgiveness.

Finally I told a friend I could not pray and I could not sleep. I expected Linda to pray for me and "make it all better." Instead she said, "Maren, stop trying. Just shut your eyes and imagine the face of God. Can you see the face of God?" Only when I said I could did she continue, "What do you see in God's face—condemnation or compassion?" She was taking a risk! "I see . . . love." "Can you accept the tenderness there, already there, in God's face, before you even ask?"

Linda offered me the face of God—no ritual formula, no particular prayers. She did not express her own opinion on the situation— whether she was shocked or thought I was overly sensitive. She said, "I offer you this gift—when you cannot forgive yourself, imagine the face of God and just see how God's looking at you."

Of course the truth is that if I had not seen forgiveness in her human face, I would not have looked any further. If I had seen judgment or impatience or dismissal or indifference or anger in the face of the friend to whom I turned—then those feelings would have reflected God for me.

What looks out of a friend's face shows us God.

—Maren

For the last five years or so, I have watched my parents try to care for their ailing parents as best they can. If one problem was taken care of, another would spring up before they had a chance to catch their breaths. My brother and I saw this, and we did our best to keep our opinions to ourselves. We listened to the laundry list of burdens our parents endured while at dinner, at the grocery store, at church to interested parishioners—anywhere and everywhere was a forum for this discussion.

The reason this is the case, I have been led to believe, is that our country now has more elderly than ever before. People are living longer, and as a result, the middle generation—the people who have finally gotten their kids out of the house and managed a few hours a day for themselves—have a new responsibility.

In our home, this got worse and worse until I felt as though I were the one spending five days a week with my grandparents, not just the one hearing about it. I brought this up with my friend Erik one evening after a particularly emotional dinner with my family. I told him that I felt guilty asking my parents to stop talking about the situation because I knew they needed release, but at the same time, it seemed like I was being robbed of any joyful or lighthearted conversations with them.

He thought about this for a while as I detailed several of the recent phone conversations I'd had that had ended with both my mother and me more depressed than before we had talked. He suggested that I tell her exactly what I had told him. When I started to protest, he said, "It's possible your parents have no idea how you feel. If that's true, it isn't fair of you to be so bitter without giving them a chance to change."

The more I considered what he said, the more I believed he was on to something. I was expecting my parents to be able to read my mind, to know that I just wanted our time together to be something that would cheer them up and give them strength when they returned to doctors' offices and sickrooms. If I could realize this about myself, then maybe they, too, would understand what I was trying to do.

—Maria

HOW HAVE FRIENDS CHALLENGED US TO GREATER SPIRITUAL MATURITY?

I have had many friends—both briefly met and long-loved. Most fit in particular niches. School friends, neighbors, clergy colleagues, and writing collaborators; my husband's cousins and my son's in-laws are friends. Many have touched me in meaningful ways. But the friends who challenged me to greater spiritual maturity are the ones I have known over a span of time, the ones who stuck it out, without benefit of wedding bells, for better and worse, rich and poor, sickness and health. Friends like that provide a challenge in two ways. When I am vulnerable and insecure, their advice challenges me to grow up, and when their lives are a shambles, they challenge me to become the helper I can be, not only in my professional life, but in my personal one as well. Recently, I have discovered a third way I have been challenged to greater spiritual maturity.

Donald and I met Donna and Keith in birth class for our older children. The young ones are also the same age, and they had a "spare" in the middle. We were friends through raising these children, with its Bethlehem of hopes and fears, through changing jobs and aging parents, as well as through less profound passages—quilting projects, vocational self-doubt, yo-yo dieting, the death of pets, the self-pity of the empty nest, bad knees, bad tempers, campfires, oven fires, a house that would not sell and a rear-end collision with five kids in the car, ten degrees below, and twenty miles from the nearest restroom. These test the mettle of friendship. Our friendship went back and forth—sometimes the phone was my life preserver in deep water, sometimes I sat all night holding the rope while Donna rappelled down some decision.

Our fathers' deaths were very different— Donna's went to sleep one night in his early seventies and did not wake up. Mine at ninety died by inches from Alzheimer's disease. At the time she was moving into a new house and getting her younger daughter ready to move to Japan. I looked for her at Dad's funeral, and she was there, like a compass. Afterward, Donna asked if I needed her to come back to the house. I realized that I did not. I was fine, spiritually mature enough, just because of the years of growing together—mature enough to let her go.

—*Maren*

During my sophomore year of college, I spent a semester in the Netherlands. My school offered a program for eighty students that allowed us to travel and study in an extension of our curriculum. We lived in a small castle built in the twelfth century, took classes together, and spent three days of every week in independent travel.

One of the two group trips was taken to Paris. All of the students taking art history that semester had a particularly rigorous schedule, but I was in the company of two of my best friends, and we planned on enjoying the sights along the way.

The first night, however, everything went wrong. Ruth and Kate were at each other's throats, and I could not keep them in better spirits. At around midnight, we ended up in front of Notre Dame, hoping to check it out before we did a joint presentation on the three portals in the morning. The plaza was still crowded, and when Kate started screaming at Ruth, nobody seemed to notice us. I tried to step in and provide a little perspective, but she turned on me instead. She told me I always sided against her and then tried to hide behind Ruth.

Both girls stormed off, and I was left in shock. I knew what Kate had told me was true. I did prefer Ruth's company to hers, and it often overbalanced the dynamic when we were all together. I had not realized, though, just how much I had been hurting her.

When I found Kate, she was standing in front of the center portal crying. I asked her forgiveness, and I thanked her for being honest with me. I could tell she did not believe me, but it was true. Until she said it to my face, I had no idea what a bad friend I was being, and there had been no way to fix what I did not know was broken.

I was lucky that night. She did forgive me, and when Ruth found us and offered no apology for her own behavior, I began to understand how deep that hurt must go. It was a blessing to have my eyes opened to my own faults because it gave me the opportunity to try again without hiding behind righteousness.

—Maria

HOW HAVE FRIENDSHIPS DEEPENED OUR FAITH?

"Ask St. Anthony." I can hear her gravely voice, "Tony will help you find it."

Originally I was the helper and Frankie the "helpee." Frankie defined herself as a leather lesbian, a cocaine addict, a dropout. The Cambridge cops called her trouble. The telephone hotline she hounded listed her as chronic caller and a pest. In religious terms an Italian Roman Catholic, Frankie promised she would talk with a Protestant woman minister, if they found her one, and get off their lines. They warned me to set boundaries. Frankie was twenty-eight at the time and I was thirty-two. She was on the brink of crippling double illnesses—one of her bones and one of her muscles—which would try to define her. For the next seventeen years I talked to Frankie. She called me and called me. If I had not heard from her in a while, I called her.

It was a phone relationship, though I remember her showing up unexpectedly at my daughter's baptism with a huge watermelon salad, the kind that is cut right into the shell. I recall, when that daughter was a preteen, Frankie told her her first "blue" joke.

Frankie had more than four hundred surgeries. Six knee replacements. Two new hips on each side. Open heart surgery many times. Shunts. Stents. Morphine patches followed by hospitalizations to break an addiction tough as street drugs. The more busted up and sewn together her body became, the stronger and funnier her spirit. She offered affection and care to staff at Brigham and Women's and Youville hospitals. She was the unofficial young wise woman of her housing project. She helped her family members who had rejected her years earlier for her sexual orientation cope with their crises.

And me? Over the hours on the phone Frankie probably gave me more advice on my ministry and my family than I ever gave her. Sometimes her advice was rough in texture. Always, it was loving in spirit.

When Frankie died at forty-five, the little funeral parlor in Somerville was packed with nurses and doctors, the wealthy and project dwellers, Catholics and Protestants—all there to testify to her courage and give thanks that she was in our lives.

Frankie, saint of lost people, find us all.

—*Maren*

I knew Rory four years before she found God. I was a sophomore in high school, she was a freshman. She was caustic and made herself lonely with a sharp tongue, but I liked that about her—she did not back down from a fight. She did not believe in anything back then, though we never discussed it. High school was not a place for deep conversations.

I went off to college, and we lost touch. I saw her at Christmas, but I did not move back after the school year ended, so the next time we talked was when I was in Europe, fall semester of my second year. She had already found God by that point. I was not there while she was looking, but she wrote me long letters about how she could not finish even one class at Stratham Tech, and she asked me to pray for her.

I prayed and I called her, but I could not keep her in school. By the time I came home, she had dropped out and she was depressed. She lost forty pounds. We ate at truck stops together and she told me how none of her friends let her talk about God. They thought her faith was more disgusting than her anorexia, than her depression. She just wanted somebody to tell her she was not the only one who heard God.

The more she told me, the more I realized I had left my faith behind when I started college. I rarely went to church, and I missed it. When I finally convinced her to move to Boston, we spent at least three days a week together. She was still depressed, but she did not shut down when we talked. Instead, she seemed to come alive telling me how she had found a Catholic church with a Latin mass.

Her faith was far from mine. Politically, we both stood the same left ground, but when it came to the church, I wanted everybody to enter in, and she felt a certain privilege that not everyone could. We argued God's law and morality, tried to decipher how close the two were, and we just kept coming back to ourselves. Our churches might not see eye to eye, but we each saw God in the other's face. It did not matter how the world twisted around us. We had a secret strength—we both heard God when we prayed.

—*Maria*

FIFTEEN

HAPPILY UNCHARTED

JAMES M. WALL

Friendship is a concept. It is also vital to our human existence, because without human relationships, of which friendship is a vital component, we simply could not ever expect to embrace life in all its fullness. I envision friendship at a human level as a conduit that connects us with the transcendent. Human friendship is a precious experience because friendship is an avenue to God. It is through friendship that we become centered in ourselves and obtain a measure of freedom to be open to God. Friendship is that elusive experience from which we view the transcendent "out of the corner of our eye" through our connection with others.

It is impossible to describe verbally, or portray visually, an encounter with God. We are left, instead, to express the awesome aftershock of grace invading our human space. It is for this reason that movies fail miserably when they attempt to portray a Jesus or God figure encountering an ordinary human. Depiction of the human Jesus on screen does not work because the viewer knows that the divine is embedded in this individual, and the man on screen cannot capture divinity.

There is one particularly painful moment in *The Greatest Story Ever Told*—a 1965 film filled with high profile stars in minor roles—in which a Roman centurion played by John Wayne utters the phrase, "Surely this man must be the Son of God." Convincing? Not at all. It is only John Wayne in first-century armor repeating a familiar phrase.

Those who know that the declaration is from the New Testament might resonate with hearing it, not because of the film, but in spite of it. In contrast, there are other grace-filled film moments that form an integral part of a secular film's narrative. These moments share, not familiar phrases, but words that address us at a deeper level within the context of the story we are experiencing.

During a scene in the 1956 film *The Searchers,* John Wayne, in a role more appropriate to his own screen image, finally finds the niece for whom he has been searching for seven years. He sees her running across the desert and rides his horse to reach her. In the film, considered by many critics to be the finest western every made, we have been led to believe that Ethan Edwards (Wayne) is so bigoted that he intends to kill his niece when he finds her because she has been living with—and is therefore defiled by—the Native American chief who kidnapped her.

When Edwards sweeps his niece Debbie (Natalie Woods) into his arms, director John Ford has him pause for a moment of uncertain tension. Then his face softens and he says quietly, "Let's go home, Debbie." In that moment of transformation Edwards allows his love for Debbie (and of her mother, a woman Edwards had loved before she was killed) to transcend his anger that had been fueled by racial bigotry and a desire for revenge.

"Let's go home, Debbie" is a spiritual moment that evokes in the viewer the experience of the power of love to transform; "Surely this must be the son of God," is a moment that only illustrated (poorly) a line from the New Testament. The difference in the two is between evoking a spiritual presence and illustrating it. And while illustration is a valid use of dialogue, it must also have the ability to evoke something beyond the words and not merely wave a flag of familiar words, trusting the audience will salute it.

God reaches us in moments of grace, and grace, by definition, is undeserved and unexpected. It is only after the fact that we can identify that the grace of God has blessed us by its presence. In viewing the film *Babette's Feast,* we think we are seeing a story of a meal prepared and consumed by surprised guests, strict religionists who think it a sin to "enjoy" worldly things like food and drink. But what is actually happening in this film are moments of grace as the dinner guests discover that the food and drink served them are actually sacramental gifts, evoking in them a sense of God's presence.

It is in this sense, then, that people like the guests at Babette's feast emerge transformed, precisely because the experience they have had introduces them to a new life. They discover that they are friends. They do not know it in the moment and, indeed, viewers of the film also do not fully grasp the significance of the transformations presented on screen. It is only in retrospect that grace as a gift from God is seen in what has otherwise appeared to be a routine story.

So it is with friendship. It is only in retrospect, sometimes years later, that we fully grasp how friendship serves as an avenue of grace from God.

Several examples of friendships in my own life come to mind. I cannot point to major events in those friendships, but can only refer to the nature of the relationships and the degree to which certain characteristics emerge that lead me to identify a connection as a friendship.

One friend that emerges in my thinking is someone I could not identify even if I wanted to because I am pledged to keep his identity a secret. So I will call him Deep Faith, which is what I called him in a series of columns I wrote in *The Christian Century* magazine.

The reason Deep Faith comes immediately to mind is that we were so different in our shared passion of electoral politics and the interaction of religion with those politics and yet we developed a sense of trust in our discussions and differences. We hardly agreed on anything intellectually, but perhaps because of the intensity of our differing perspectives, we achieved a connection that transcended human disagreements. Over a period of time we formed a bond built on our conversations while we shared a commuter train from our suburban homes to the city of Chicago.

Because I wanted my friend to speak freely about our differences, which I would then report in my columns, I agreed not to identify him to my readers. That way he would be protected from his colleagues in the religious and political arenas. That was important because Deep Faith is a very conservative religious Protestant (did anyone mention charismatic?) and he was a political conservative in the Ronald Reagan mold—not mean and mendacious, but committed to a philosophically conservative solution to national and international problems. He was also a Christian who believed in conservative religious traditions.

As I reflect back on our time together it makes all the sense in the world to me to refer back to Deep Faith in any discussion on friendship. I believe that one important characteristic required for friendship is compatibility, the experience of "getting along" at a level of respect, comfort, and a desire to engage the other in matters of common interest. Friendships that resonate at a level deep enough to lead us into a higher spiritual realm must be built on these characteristics; otherwise they become shared experiences that are not anchored in common values of compatibility and respect.

A second characteristic needed in the building of friendships is trust, the certainty that a friend will stand by you, regardless. Trust is earned over time through experience and through that strange sense we have in our relationships that this is someone on whom I can rely, and I believe that the same feeling is shared by my friend.

I have another friend whose political views are perhaps even more disparate from my own, a politician and public relations professional with whom I have shared many a conversation (and total disagreements) on a multitude of issues, political and religious. What brings this friend immediately to mind is the memory of something he once said to a colleague of ours when he was asked what it was that made two such disparate characters feel, in spite of our differences, such a bond of friendship. My friend responded: "Jim is the friend of mine I would most want to have walking with me should I drop to the sidewalk with a heart attack."

He was certainly not suggesting that I would have any medical expertise to be of help to him in such a circumstance. Far from it; medical matters make me queasy. But I accepted his comment to mean that when he went down, either permanently or temporarily, he would like me to be there with him. Why? I am not sure, but my guess is that in moments of crisis, we do not want to be alone. And even when we are surrounded by a crowd of people, it is important that at least one in the crowd is a trusted friend.

A third friend of mine is a person with whom I spent more than eight years riding bikes together along a path through our county. Our trips were usually on the weekends, though on occasion we would slip out in the late afternoon during the summer before dusk to cover four to six miles along the path. On those rides, we talked ourselves into moments of deep sharing, as Kris Kristofferson puts it, sharing the "secrets" of our souls.

This friend did actually hit the sidewalk with me by his side on one occasion. We were out on a cold New Year's Day, walking, not riding, as the ice made riding impossible. Along one stretch of sidewalk, my friend slipped on the ice and fell down, hard. I think of this incident because it reminds me that a third characteristic of friendship, after compatibility and trust, is humor. A shared sense of what is funny in that relationship.

As my friend lay on the ice, in obvious pain, I told him, "Get up, man, you look ridiculous." I think he said something equally inane, but my comment was intended to relieve the tension of the moment and humor—a completely inappropriate comment designed to bring a smile—was my effort to let him know I was there.

Fortunately, a jogger came along more interested in helping than being funny, and she volunteered to go across the street to phone for an ambulance. She did, and my friend and I ended up at the local hospital. I called his wife, who came immediately, and I soon departed, once it became clear that my friend had broken his leg. He has never let me forget—and he will tell all who will listen, like an Ancient Mariner—that I laughed at him in his misery.

When I saw the superb motion picture *Capote*, which examines the author Truman Capote's research and writing for his book *In Cold Blood*, I was struck by the friendship that emerged in that film. I do not refer to the friendship between Capote and the murderer Perry Smith, on whom the homosexual Capote developed a crush and whom he exploited to obtain information for his book. That connection could be examined as an example of how relationships are distorted for ulterior motives by one or both of the partners. Everyone who pays attention can recall moments when it becomes apparent that what we thought was a friendship was in fact a mere connection through which one or both individuals had been "using" the other for emotional gain.

The friendship I followed in *Capote* was the strong relationship between Capote and his friend from childhood, Harper Lee, the author of the book *To Kill A Mockingbird*. In *Capote* Harper Lee is portrayed by the actress Catherine Keener, who travels with Capote to the site of four murders in Kansas, serving as both research partner and companion.

As Harper Lee, Keener is the friend without whom Capote could not have successfully researched or written his book. She is clearly devoted to him. The early years of the relationship are chronicled in her novel, *To Kill a Mockingbird*, when the young neighbor boy, "Dill," representing Truman Capote as a child, is shown as Scout's (Harper's) childhood friend.

Director Bennett Miller and screenwriters Dan Futterman and Gerald Clark refer to Lee's own writing career only in passing in their film, but it is clear that they see her as a pivotal companion for Capote, a man much in need of a friend who understands and accepts his eccentric ways. Capote is a controlling, arrogant, and highly creative writer who becomes obsessed with the murder story onto which he stumbled after reading about it in a New York City newspaper. He travels to Kansas to interview anyone who can help him understand the crime that took the lives of a family of four. He will not go without Lee, for she is not only his research helper, she is also his emotional anchor as he ventures outside the protective (for an openly gay man) environment of New York City's salon life.

Lee gives her friend stern advice, presents him with options, and forces him to take whatever action he, as the creative writer, deems best. She stands by him even as his behavior is, in her judgment, wrong. Capote complicates his task, especially as he begins to develop a strong affection for one of the killers. Harper does not like the manner in which Capote, as an author, exploits his "source" in the murder. But she also knows that Capote's book will not be finished until he has obtained an eyewitness account of the manner in which a failed robbery elevated into four senseless killings.

"Friends don't let friends drink and drive" is a wise saying. Friends must decide just how much negative behavior they will tolerate in a friend. And that need for a realistic awareness of how damaging, or perhaps, creative, wrongful behavior can be in a friend brings us back to another important characteristic of a good friend: The ability to identify the negative in a friend and to force that friend to consider the effect of his or her behavior. In the film version of the Lee-Capote relationship Lee is the stronger of the two, standing by Capote as he agonizes in his lengthy struggle to write the book that will become a classic in American literature. Friendship must exist on that narrow ledge between what is best and what is right.

Everyone should be as fortunate as Capote to have a friend as available with her openness and candor as Harper Lee. Was this openness and sharing true about the two of them in real life? I have no idea, but we have the film's interpretation of the strength of their friendship, which is a good example of what psychologists might describe as the dependency of two people on one another, one strong, the other weak in the realm of human maturity (though in terms of creativity, Truman probably had the edge).

Is it healthy for one person to have to prop up another to get him or her through agonizing moments of ambiguous behavior? Perhaps not, but many creative people are not emotionally healthy to begin with, which is often what drives them in their creativity. And friendships are as varied as the individuals who form them. We do not look for, nor should we expect to find, perfect friendships. Our task here, rather, is to identify the characteristics on which friendships are built.

And as I write about Capote and Lee, my mind opens on a small window of memory, which reminds me that friendships need not always be between two individuals over a long period of time. There are instances of friendship that sparkle in our lives and then we move on, forever grateful for what we have encountered, fully knowing the experience was ours for that moment, not as something that builds between two individuals, but as one person reaching out to help another in a time of need.

The memory that flashes before me was a crisis moment during the 1972 Democratic National Convention in Miami, Florida. I was the chairman of the George McGovern delegation from Illinois, about a third of the delegation members. Through a bit of manipulation from the campaign manager, Gary Hart, the Illinois vote for McGovern on the convention floor was arranged so that Illinois would be the state that delivered the nomination to McGovern.

We were all a bit giddy to have that honor and as I walked away from a convention session a little later, I was asked by a Chicago reporter what I thought of McGovern's choice of a vice-presidential nominee. His selection of Missouri senator Tom Eagleton came as a complete surprise to me. The choice of Eagleton had not reached our delegation. Ever the eager one to respond to reporters' questions, I stammered a bit, and then felt a hand on my arm. It was a woman about my age who was a member of the Illinois delegation (I regret that I no longer remember her name, but I can still see her face, calm, resolute, and firm). She asked me to step over to the corner of the room, where she suggested that I find out more about Eagleton before I offered any answers.

She was right, of course, and in that moment she was the best friend I had in Miami. I excused myself from the reporter and found Illinois senator Adlai Stevenson, who knew Eagleton and who, in two minutes, gave me a reassuring summary of why McGovern had chosen a good running mate. (When it emerged later that Eagleton had received treatment for an emotional condition, he was in my opinion, unfairly forced to leave the ticket.)

I returned to my questioner and gave him Stevenson's summary opinion (now my own) as to what was good about the Eagleton selection. My friend of the moment, the young female delegate, stood by with a smile. She had made sure that for that instant, at least, we would have a positive spin on our vice-presidential media story. She was not, of course, merely acting as my friend of the moment. She also wanted to make sure I did not harm the McGovern campaign, which suggests that no act of friendship need be pure to qualify as a positive contribution.

When occasions like this return to consciousness, we are uplifted into a realm of thankfulness. Hence, another characteristic of a friend is to be present to others at all times, ever ready to reach out with a helping word, admonition, or just plain act of assistance.

I began these reflections with a cinematic example of the transforming power of friendship. I will close with some words from a poet of loneliness and friendship, Kris Kristofferson, who began his career as a country music songwriter in Nashville. Some of Kristofferson's finest work has focused on the intimate connection between loneliness and friendship. Without friends, loneliness is a constant companion. Our darkest moments come when we feel deserted.

Kristofferson starts his song of love and friendship, *Me and Bobby McGee*, by placing us in the moment when the singer and his traveling companion are "busted flat in Baton Rouge and headed for the train." The poet and the girl he loves, Bobby McGee, are friends and companions as well as lovers. They share a conviction that "freedom's just another word for nothing left to lose; nothing ain't worth nothing but it's free," a description of existential angst and longing that would have had even Søren Kierkegaard tapping his foot along with them.

The poet declares that Bobby shared the "secrets of my soul," as the two travel from the "coal mines of Kentucky to the California sun," which is what friendship is all about, soul-sharing, when you think about it. It was also the reason why "feeling good was good enough when Bobby sang the blues." Of course, it could not last; that is what the blues are all about, dreams deferred and lost. Nor are we surprised that "somewhere near Salinas, Lord, I let her slip away, looking for the home I hope she'll find." Where is that home? Bobby McGee has had glimpses of what she is seeking through her friendship with the poet.

Love and friendship are too powerful to be grasped except by inference and sharing. That which is left is a permeating and transcendent reality, which is why our poet can sing that "nothing left" in this life leaves him with a longing. Very much implied in his poetry is the realization that what is left for us to cherish are the shadows of what was and will be. And of that we will tell stories, and make movies, and write folk songs.

It was grace that got the poet through that dark night somewhere close to Salinas. And it was grace that inspired the poet to write his song. So it is with those of us who try and write "about" friendship. You cannot do it, you know, because friendship is such a powerful connection to the transcendent that to describe it is to let it slip away. Which is precisely why we must discuss friendship the way we show God and grace in the movies, or sing it in folk songs, or describe it in our lives. They are realities sparkling just out of the corner of our eyes. As Peter Falk says to an angel who hovers about him in the movie *Wings of Desire*, "I can't see you, but I know you are there."

SIXTEEN

FRIENDS WHO HARVEST HOPE

JOE A. WILSON

I was only a young boy in my early teens when I was awakened one night by voices of sadness coming from the living room of our home. I slipped through the doorway and saw the father and son who lived next door consoling each other. The room was filled with grief.

Slowly, with the help of my mother, I put the pieces together. There had been a terrible accident. The mother of the family next door had been killed on a rain slick highway to Beaumont. Jimmy, my best friend, had lost his mother, a warm tender lady who so many times had offered me the gracious hospitality of her home. She, in a sense, was a second mother of love for me.

The reality of that experience set in motion a series of questions in my life that eventually guided me to the Methodist Youth Fellowship at First Methodist Church (no "United" at that time) in Orange, Texas. It was there that I found a marvelous young couple, Virginia and Sandy, who were counselors for the youth. They listened to my questions, cradled my teenage fears, and made a skinny, fifteen-year-old boy feel a sense of worth. As they nurtured me in my first close encounter with death, I was introduced for the first time to a God of infinite love, who did not abandon us at times of death or other catastrophes in life. Without the use of lofty theology, they helped me become acquainted with a God who is closer than breath and cares about the minor and major concerns of my heart. It was out of these conversations that I developed a regular prayer life as a teenager. To this day, I have fond memories of praying nightly, on my knees in my chocolate brown bedroom, leaning against a blond-colored twin bed. I believe that God rested a gentle spirit within my heart during those nightly conversations of prayer, and this simple invasion eventually led me to a commitment to ordained ministry.

Over the length of fifty years, Virginia and Sandy have continued to be a strong presence in the life of the same congregation. They have suffered the loss of a child and the addiction of another but have never wavered in their faith and consistent loyalty to the church where they guided many young persons into stronger faith.

The next three years I seldom missed those Sunday night Methodist Youth Fellowship meetings. They set a stirring inside of me, and I began to experience a community of support and love. In the second year of this journey, I responded on Sunday evening to the invitation of Pastor Morgan. He did not have a great gift of preaching, but his loving presence led me to be baptized and join the church. My eventual decision to enter the vocation of ordained ministry was influenced by a combination of God's tugging Spirit and Pastor Morgan's persistent pushes. I would go to Sunday morning services in fear, knowing that Pastor Morgan would ask me to read the scripture, give a morning prayer, or say the benediction, without any early warning. I nervously sat through the service with my finger in the section of the hymnal where prayers and benedictions were printed, just to make me feel safe. During this time I was elected president of the youth fellowship, and Pastor Morgan believed that youth leaders should be given leadership responsibilities. Although I never admitted it, he built a fear on Sunday mornings that almost convinced me that if a minister had to do this every Sunday, I could not be one.

This passing fear, however, was soon absorbed through familiarity, as I am sure the pastor wisely knew would happen. I accepted God's and Pastor Morgan's call to preach and gave my first sermon in the pulpit that had terrorized me for years. This is the same pulpit to which I returned to preach my first sermon after being elected a bishop. I am sure there was a marked difference in the quality and length of the two sermons. My high school English teacher was present as this seventeen-year-old boy struggled through ten of the longest minutes of his life. After I gave birth to my sermon with a great sigh of relief, my English teacher offered a chilling critique: "If you are going to be a preacher, don't use the words, 'You know' twenty-four times in a sermon, and remember the word 'often' is pronounced with a silent 't'." That was the first of many helpful comments from the pew that have improved my preaching over the years. Two other post-sermon remarks, given in my early churches, are printed in my mind with vivid memory: "Pastor, I was with you to the bitter end" and "Sure was glad it was short."

These "holy friendships" led me closer to God in those years of early formation. I could not have grown through teenage insecurities without the loving care of Virginia and Sandy, Pastor Morgan, and yes, even a high school English teacher. The caring presence of two devoted counselors, the gentle pushes that sometimes became shoves of a forceful pastor, and the critique of a well-meaning teacher, all shaped the early roots of my spiritual life. They taught me important lessons in the young years of my faith discoveries and helped me find hope and courage tempered with resiliency. They gave innocence and immaturity a welcoming acceptance, with a few harsh realignments, and thereby created a willingness to take a journey of faith.

In the years that followed there were many who shaped my spiritual life as I embarked on the adventure of growing a more informed faith. My university and seminary experience brought friends who molded an intellectual dimension into my spiritual journey. These friends were not so protective of my youthful ideals, but challenged me with uncomfortable questions asked for rational reasons.

In those years, I learned that feeling good about a great God of love and acceptance could be thrown off balance with serious questions of theological dialogue. One such friend was a professor of philosophy at my university. He also served as the supervisor of my dorm, which made it convenient to engage him in conversations. Another young student, who is now a renowned professor of ethics at a prestigious seminary, and I often tried out our theories of theological solutions. These were great moments of mind expansion that led to fulfilling discoveries. On one occasion Stanley and I had worked all week on a theory of salvation that in our minds solved the problems of predestination, universal acceptance, world religions, and an assortment of other difficult questions. We rushed to explain it to our friend John, whom we assumed would see it as a theological breakthrough. He listened patiently and then said, "Where is the central doctrine of Christology?" Oops! We had dug so deeply in the grey matter of rationalization that we left behind our Christian roots. John gently repackaged our ideas and helped us grow a foot taller in theological integrity that night.

Friends who are willing to listen to your shallow conclusions and build upon them with firm insights are helpful guides in the years of faith construction. Professor John gave this gift to me. His chuckle was never meant to embarrass or demean my struggle, but it brought a relaxed safety into our conversation. I knew I could ask any superficial question and offer any doltish conclusion, without feeling rejected or unimportant. That quality reflected in John has helped me tolerate some of the most misdirected inquiries over the years with a listening heart and a gentle gift of reconstruction.

Seminary brought a friend who was not so committed to preserving my feelings of safety. This professor attacked my first paper with a bottle of red ink. He visited the library and retrieved all the quotes that I had failed to identity and marked them with insulting accusations of plagiarism. It was a great lesson learned. This friend helped me see the value of creative individualism, which I applied thereafter.

The friendships that develop in the seminary days of intellectual growth are often remembered with great appreciation in later years. As a potter creates a vase with fire and tender touches, these friendships are those that give foundations to our mental understandings with the same kind of encounter. So many of the secure planks in our well-built castles of truth suddenly weaken under the barrage of questions. The teacher, like a potter, throws our ill-formed shapes into the fire and we first hurt with the heat of doubt. Then, like a master craftsman, the teacher brings us to life again with dependable thoughts and reliable theology.

These friends, who shared wisdom and faith in seminary days, have been some of the most valuable in my life. In the beginning I experienced a collapse of what I thought were perfectly dependable limbs of theological thought. Under the weight of new ideas and the pruning of old ones, I found a more secure faith. Deschner, Ogden, Outler, Harvey, Allen, Furnish, Power and so many others became for me the "hounds of heaven." They barked at the heels of complacency and forced me to work through my doubts. I remember a rather devastating paper with one word across the first page: "Bull!" The times when I wanted to hide from such direct critiques and when anger, along with despair, filled my being, were also the times of my greatest growth. I learned to face these inevitable criticisms and befriend them as they forced me to regroup and pursue a higher scholarship. I will always be grateful for these friends.

After graduation with a respectable grade-point, I discovered how valuable these friends had been for my soul. A young church, to which I was assigned, experienced a charismatic revival shortly before I arrived. Many of the congregation were brought closer to Christ, and I discovered a loving spirit among a number of the members. But the theology being spread by the leaders began to threaten the majority of the flock with self-doubt and judgment. Because of the foundations of thought supplied by my seminary professor friends, I was able to stand firm without self-doubt, teach a more reliable Christology, and bring a disturbed church back to the center. Though it was necessary for some of the members to leave, the majority stayed with a renewed commitment and love for one another. The gifts of these seminary professors and the foundations they laid in my life have been built upon through the years. I have traveled, in some cases, to an expanded and more developed level of thought, but I have always kept with deep appreciation the abiding, life-shaping truths I learned at their feet.

As I entered the post-seminary chapter of my life and took on the role of a pastor, I discovered a new level of friendships. Many of my friends became those for whom I was given the responsibility of pastoral care. Unlike my seminary experiences, I became the friend who was there in times of joy and sadness. I walked with those who were lost and broken. I rescued friends who were lonely. I guided those who were hungry for new life. However, out of this level of friendship, I realized that I was protecting my own vulnerability, lest I be not strong and insightful for those who needed me. There was a cautious distance I kept between these friends and my inner feelings. If I depended too much on a friend, I thought I could not be the rescuer, the counselor, the shepherd.

A word needs to be said about this self-imposed isolation. It is a danger that causes the burn-out and burn-up of many pastors. Where does a pastor go to find a friend? Must friendships always be burdened in the pastor's life with a limited exposure of his or her own pain and suffering? What will people think if they find out that their pastor has a weakness or a heart-rending human burden? Will they listen to him as a preacher? Will they go to her as a counselor? What a strain this isolation also puts on the pastor's spouse. Is there no one who can hear her or his human struggles with confidentiality and insight?

Along with restriction regarding the pastor's image, the vocation of ordained ministry can promote another suffocating belief as it relates to friends. It is the idea that one must not become too close with any family in the church, lest the congregation grow jealous or feel that the pastor has favorites. This also restrained my life and that of my family in my first appointed churches.

I am thankful, however, for a whole collection of friends who eliminated these myths of pastoral leadership. I remember Joe Bill and Mildred, who perceived our loneliness in a town of a thousand residents. On a weekly basis they took us to eat one of Dolly's hamburgers at the cotton-gin café and always made sure my wife was included in any social event or trip to the big city. I recall John and Cindy, who made their home a place of delightful meals and who, even with ill health, continued to include us in many family events. I remember Lee and Sylvia, with whom we felt the comfort of relaxation and laughter and who gave us permission to just be ourselves in their understanding presence. Over the years these friendships melted down the stuffy status of a "position" and made our lives rich with love and acceptance. Without these friends, we could have lost the joy of ministry, suffocating in the thin air of pedestal sitting.

Before leaving this collection of friendships, I must mention Scotty and Linda. There are some friends in the ministry that one never forgets because they are the ones who made you temporarily leave your "post" and splash in the waters with your children. Scotty, a busy space-center scientist, insisted that I play with my kids. He pulled me into scouting, Indian Princesses, derby racing, horseback riding, camping, and many other activities that took precious time from the demands of a large church. He helped me see that ministry would still be there long after my children were gone. He and Linda were friends who refocused our priorities and, in such an adjustment, became friends for life. They helped us know the sheer excitement of just stopping and playing with the family. They would not take no for an answer and saved me from many evenings of a perceived demand of "have to" responsibilities. Today, Linda is fighting a life-threatening battle with bone cancer, and Scotty is faithfully by her side. I am sure they in their redirected lives have no regrets about their investment of time. Even with heavy responsibilities, they played with their kids, and these two dear friends taught me the importance of that priority.

One cannot travel too far into life without encountering friends who support you when your heart is breaking. These are the friends who seem to always know your needs, and, without asking, they know what to do. My wife and I have not suffered the painful loss of children in death. However, we have felt the loss of dreams we had for them. We have known the heartbreak that comes when children disappoint you. This disappointment came in the form of an early wedding of our daughter, prompted by an unexpected pregnancy. Although her two-year union ended with a divorce, we celebrate today three fine grandsons from our daughter's present marriage, as well as the beautiful granddaughter the first marriage produced. Even though there was joy in the morning, the darkness of the night before filled our hearts with sadness.

It was during this darkness that we found the supporting love of friendships of those who did not ask questions but just did what we found hard to do. Within a short time a wonderful shower was given by friends. A lovely wedding was planned by friends who wanted to affirm and not judge two young kids as they began a new life together. I will never forget Marge, Jack, Patricia, Julie, Ross, and so many more who reached above a heartbreak and gave us a gift of loving friendship. It is in these friendships that one discovers the nature of God's unrelenting love. Over the years these friends have remained constant in our lives. I believe that, by walking through this painful experience with us, they connected their own humanity with ours and we learned that we belong to one another.

Though friends provide care and nourishment in times of great need, I have also experienced the disappointment of friends. I think it is important to reflect upon when one must let a friendship die. Do we keep friends for life and overlook tragic betrayals in the relationship? Is there a friendship loyalty code that encourages us to accept any behavior from a friend?

When friends have betrayed you or their lifestyle is unacceptable, it is difficult to give up a once valued relationship. I remember two friends in my early ministry. We served neighboring churches and our families enjoyed evenings together. After a few years, a sad divorce separated these two friends and the male friend accepted a pastoral appointment in another state. We remained close to both. As the years advanced and I became a bishop, my old friend asked for a ministerial appointment in the state where I was assigned. Not long afterward I had the opportunity to offer the male friend, who had remarried, an appointment to a splendid church. He had been successful in the churches he had served in another state, and I rejoiced in this anticipated renewal of an old friendship. Within two years he had betrayed my trust, and his ministerial credentials were taken away. What do you do with a friendship destroyed by unacceptable behavior? Is forgiveness always appropriate? So many different circumstances dictate the response. However, in this case, I concluded that friendship cannot be built on dishonesty. Sometimes a rift can be irreparable when the friendship has been used for selfish gains and truthfulness rejected. Friendships cannot always endure secrecies that threaten the well-being of the other party. Like beautiful flowers, friendships grow in light, not in darkness. They are the product of genuine trust.

As I bring this chapter to the end, I must share with you the story of one of my best friends, who happens to be my son. Paul is our adopted son, and his life has not always been easy. Through a genetic inheritance he was placed in this world with bipolar disorder. As Paul was growing up as a young teenager, he knew of no other way to ease the pain of this terrible condition except through alcohol. Unaware of his struggle and the reasons for his alcohol consumption, we were not able to get him adequate treatment. As a result, he did not receive the medical attention needed and, after a try at college, he entered the Navy. For the next ten years Paul bravely endured the hardships of military life combined with the vagaries of his bipolar condition. His journey has been filled with difficult hurdles but he has faced them with courage.

Paul has now received treatment for his condition and lives his life with a thankful joy, remembering the days when he was suicidal and filled with uncontrollable anxiety. He lives within the parameters of his limitations and has become a deeply caring person, feeling the pain of others more sensitively than those of us who have not experienced the hardships of a mental disorder.

The reason I mention this friendship is that it, unlike a betrayed friendship, is a restored friendship growing out of disappointment and frustration. As parents, the earlier lifestyle of our son caused much resentment and sometimes anger. Jobs were short-term, college was a failure, marriage ended in divorce. No amount of reasoning brought change, and all of our emotional support seemed to make little difference.

Then one day, this son came home. He entered rehabilitation. He found the right combination of medicines for his bipolar condition. He moved to the town where we live and began to venture back into life. We reached out with gentle help, giving him support where needed. He offered a new honesty and trustworthiness. With his added anxiety disorder, there are still places my son can never go and things he will never be able to do, but that is okay. I rejoice in his kind nature, his generosity, his returned humor, his patience, and his desire to ease the pain of so many. We see each other every day and enjoy the presence of a restored friendship. I trust him and believe in him.

The greatest friendship one can have is a friendship that is restored and replenished with honesty and respect for each other. For this is like the friendship humankind shares with the Creator. A broken condition is aggravated by deception and failed attempts to care for the pain of separation. But with the grace of acceptance and genuine trust, we find peace in the arms of an embracing God. Friendship then blossoms into new life and we live again in a newfound harmony. It is not a friendship that is perfect, for we still carry the dust of a fallen creation. But its beauty lies in a restoration filled with honesty and hope. Friendships are truly holy when they are built with the architecture of God's plan. The relationship with my son is a holy friendship in which I have learned lessons of grace and restoration not unlike the lessons of friendship I have experienced with God.

CONTRIBUTORS

Esther Kwon Arinaga is a retired public interest lawyer. A member of a United Methodist congregation in Hawaii for more than seven decades, she continues to be active in her community with social and political issues. Her essays have appeared in six books and various journals.

James Armstrong is a retired United Church of Christ minister. Currently teaching at Rollins College and the Florida Center for Theological Studies, Armstrong is a former United Methodist bishop. He served as president of the National Council of Churches in the 1980s and was president of the Florida Council of Churches in the mid-1990s. He is author of ten books, the most recent *Feet of Clay on Solid Ground* (BookSurge, 2002).

Paschal Baumstein is a Benedictine monk and Catholic priest at Belmont Abbey in North Carolina. Working as an intellectual historian, his publications have focused on Anselm and other medievals. He is a former book editor of the monastic journal *Cistercian Studies Quarterly*.

Gilbert H. Caldwell retired as senior minister of the Park Hill United Methodist Church in Denver in 2001, after serving forty-five years in the ministry. His clergy service includes churches in Massachusetts,

Connecticut, New York (Brooklyn and Harlem), Pennsylvania, and Colorado. A founder and former president of Black Methodists for Church Renewal, he recently helped form the United Methodists of Color for a Fully Inclusive Church. His recently published book, *What Mean These Stones? Lessons of Hurricane Katrina, 9/11, the Million Man March, the Millions More Movement* (iUniverse, 2005), reflects his effort to take seriously Karl Barth's words: "The Christian lives life with the Bible in one hand and the newspaper in the other."

Kenneth L. Carder is professor of the practice of pastoral formation at Duke Divinity School, Durham, North Carolina. He served as bishop of the Nashville Area of the United Methodist Church from 1992 to 2000, and the Jackson (Mississippi) Area from 2000 to 2004. Prior to his election to the episcopacy from Church Street United Methodist Church in Knoxville, he pastored congregations in Tennessee and Virginia. He is the author of four books and several articles, and he has preached and lectured throughout the United States and in Africa, Europe, and Asia.

Musa W. Dube is associate professor of New Testament at the University of Botswana in southern Africa. As a theological consultant for the World Council of Churches and theological institutions in Africa, she has traveled the continent speaking and providing workshops on HIV and AIDS. Holding a Ph.D. from Vanderbilt University, Dube taught at Scripps College in California as a visiting scholar. She is the author of *Postcolonial Feminist Interpretations of the Bible* (Chalice Press, 2000) and she coedited two other books, *Grant Me Justice! HIV/AIDS & Gender Readings of the Bible* (Orbis, 2003) and *Other Ways of Reading: African Women and the Bible* (SBI, 2002).

Vince Isner is the director of FaithfulAmerica.org, a D.C.-based inter-faith e-advocacy organization of the National Council of Churches, engaging more than a hundred thousand persons in addressing public policy issues from a progressive interreligious perspective. A twenty-five-year veteran in communications, Vince has served on Capitol Hill as a communications director, hosted his own children's program, served as a Minister to Children and Families, and, through his production company, produced and directed dozens of international documentaries and study courses.

Kathleen LaCamera is a print, television, and radio journalist whose award-winning work has taken her around the globe for U.S. and European publications and broadcasters. Her special interest in divided communities has led her to report on the troubles in Northern Ireland, the war in Bosnia, and racism in the United States and the United Kingdom. She is a recent contributor to *Creating America: Reading and Writing Arguments* and *Global Exchange: Reading and Writing in a World Context*, both published by Prentice Hall (2005). An ordained minister with standing in both the U.S. and British Methodist churches, she also consults and lectures on issues related to communication, media, and theology.

Martin E. Marty is the Fairfax M. Cone Distinguished Service Professor Emeritus at the University of Chicago, where he taught, chiefly in the Divinity School, for thirty-five years and where the Martin Marty Center has since been founded to promote "public religion" endeavors. He is a Lutheran clergyman and columnist for *The Christian Century*, on whose staff he has served since 1956. He is a regular contributor to *Sightings*, a biweekly, electronic editorial published by the Marty Center. Dr. Marty is the author of more than fifty books, including *Righteous Empire*, for which he won the National Book Award.

Stephen K. McCeney has a doctorate in counseling psychology and is a licensed clinical and school psychologist. He has worked as a psychotherapist and consultant for more than twenty years in a variety of settings, including hospitals, mental health centers, universities, large corporations, private practice, and schools. Dr. McCeney is currently working as a school psychologist for the Denver public schools and has a part-time private practice where he specializes in gay and lesbian issues, relationships, chronic and terminal illnesses, and depression.

Donald E. Messer, president emeritus and former Henry White Warren Professor of Practical Theology at Iliff School of Theology, Denver, Colorado, is president of the Center for the Church and Global AIDS. The Center engages the church constructively in the struggle against global HIV/AIDS. Speaking and leading workshops has taken him to more than thirty countries around the world. The most recent of his eleven books include *Breaking the Conspiracy of Silence: Christian Churches and the Global AIDS Crisis* (Augsburg Fortress, 2004) and *Ending Hunger Now: A Challenge to Persons of Faith* (Augsburg Fortress, 2005) with former Senators George McGovern and Bob Dole.

M. Kent Millard is lead pastor at St. Luke's United Methodist Church in Indianapolis, Indiana, which is a fifty-six-hundred-member congregation with thirty-two hundred persons in worship in ten different services each week. His vision is to renew the church for the sake of the transformation of the world, and he has led his congregation to give away about $1.2 million each year in outreach ministries to help the world become AIDS-free, hunger free, and prejudice free. His most recent book is entitled *The Passion Driven Congregation* (Abingdon, 2003), which he coauthored with his predecessor, Dr. Carver McGriff. He and his wife, Minnietta, have two children and seven grandchildren.

Donna Schaper is the senior minister of Judson Memorial Church in New York City. She is the author of twenty-two books, most recently *Sacred Speech* (Skylight Paths, 2004), *Holy Vulnerability* (ACTA Publications, 2005), and *Mature Grief* (Cowley, 2003). She takes a train up to Kingston, New York, often, especially in the fall, winter, spring, and summer.

Karen Stone is an artist and art educator. She has shown her work in local, national, and international exhibitions and has artworks in more than thirty private and public collections. She received her Master of Fine Arts degree from Arizona State University. At present she is adjunct professor of art at the University of Texas at Arlington and art specialist for the Fort Worth schools. Her most recent book was *Image and Spirit: Finding Meaning in Visual Art* (Augsburg Books, 2003). She has presented workshops on the subject of art and spirituality in the United States, South America, Africa, and Great Britian. She lives with Howard, her husband of more than forty years, and enjoys her daughter, son-in-law, and two granddaughters.

Maren C. Tirabassi is a poet, liturgical writer, and United Church of Christ pastor who has served six churches in Massachusetts and New Hampshire over the past twenty-five years. She is the author or editor of eleven books, most recently *Faith Made Visible* (United Church Press, 2000), *Blessing New Voices* (Pilgrim Press, 2000), and *Transgendering Faith* (Pilgrim Press, 2004). She also teaches the writing of poetry and memoir.

Maria I. Tirabassi is a poet, liturgical writer, and preschool teacher who recently graduated from Emerson College with a Bachelor of Fine Arts in writing, literature, and publishing. She is the author/editor of several books, including her most recent, *Day Book for New Voices* (Pilgrim Press, 2004). Forthcoming from Pilgrim Press is *Caring for Ourselves While Caring for Our Elders* (in press).

James M. Wall is senior contributing editor for *The Christian Century* magazine, based in Chicago, Illinois. From 1972 to 1999, he was editor and publisher of the magazine. He is a United Methodist clergyman.

Joe A. Wilson served as the United Methodist bishop of the Central Texas Conference from 1992 to 2000. Prior to his election to the episcopacy, he was senior pastor at Marvin United Methodist Church, Tyler, Texas, and Provost of the Texas Annual Conference. He has received the Distinguished Alumni Award from both his seminary, Perkins School of Theology, and his university, Southwestern University, where he now serves as bishop-in-residence.